Postmodern Philosophical Critique *and the* Pursuit of Knowledge in Higher Education

Critical Studies in Education and Culture Series

Repositioning Feminism and Education: Perspective on Educating for Social Change
*Janice Jipson, Petra Munro, Susan Victor, Karen Froude Jones,
and Gretchen Freed-Rowland*

Culture, Politics, and Irish School Dropouts: Constructing Political Identities
G. Honor Fagan

Anti-Racism, Feminism, and Critical Approaches to Education
Roxana Ng, Pat Staton, and Joyce Scane

Beyond Comfort Zones in Multiculturalism: Confronting the Politics of Privilege
Sandra Jackson and José Solís, editors

Culture and Difference: Critical Perspectives on the Bicultural Experience in the United States
Antonia Darder

Poststructuralism, Politics and Education
Michael Peters

Weaving a Tapestry of Resistance: The Places, Power, and Poetry of a Sustainable Society
Sharon Sutton

Counselor Education for the Twenty-First Century
Susan J. Brotherton

Positioning Subjects: Psychoanalysis and Critical Educational Studies
Stephen Appel

Adult Students "At-Risk": Culture Bias in Higher Education
Timothy William Quinnan

Education and the Postmodern Condition
Michael Peters, editor

Restructuring for Integrative Education: Multiple Perspectives, Multiple Contexts
Todd E. Jennings, editor

Postmodern Philosophical Critique *and the* Pursuit of Knowledge in Higher Education

ROGER P. MOURAD, JR.

Critical Studies in Education and Culture Series
Edited by Henry A. Giroux

BERGIN & GARVEY
Westport, Connecticut • London

Library of Congress Cataloging-in-Publication Data

Mourad, Roger P. (Roger Philip), 1958–
  Postmodern philosophical critique and the pursuit of knowledge in higher education / Roger P. Mourad, Jr.
    p. cm.—(Critical studies in education and culture series, ISSN 1064–8615)
  Includes bibliographical references and index.
  ISBN 0–89789–488–X (alk. paper). ISBN 0–89789–554–1 (pbk.)
  1. Education, Higher—Philosophy. 2. Postmodernism and education.
  3. Inquiry (Theory of knowledge) 4. Research—Philosophy.
  I. Title. II. Series.
  LB2322.2.M68 1997
  378′.001—dc21   97–217

British Library Cataloguing in Publication Data is available.

Copyright © 1997 by Roger P. Mourad, Jr.

All rights reserved. No portion of this book may be reproduced, by any process or technique, without the express written consent of the publisher.

Library of Congress Catalog Card Number: 97–217
ISBN: 0–89789–488–X
      0–89789–554–1 (pbk.)
ISSN: 1064–8615

First published in 1997

Bergin & Garvey, 88 Post Road West, Westport, CT 06881
An imprint of Greenwood Publishing Group, Inc.

Printed in the United States of America

The paper used in this book complies with the Permanent Paper Standard issued by the National Information Standards Organization (Z39.48–1984).

P

> In order to keep this title in print and available to the academic community, this edition was produced using digital reprint technology in a relatively short print run. This would not have been attainable using traditional methods. Although the cover has been changed from its original appearance, the text remains the same and all materials and methods used still conform to the highest book-making standards.

For my dear sons, Julian and Theo

I love learning with you

Contents

Series Foreword by Henry A. Giroux	ix
Preface	xiii
1. Introduction: Modern Inquiry and Postmodern Critique	1
2. The Modern Foundations of Progress in the Pursuit of Knowledge	11
3. Lyotard, Rorty, and Schrag: The Search for New Grounds for Inquiry	27
4. Foucault and Derrida: Inquiry as Intellectual Activity that Acts Upon and Changes Reality	55
5. Past, Present, and Possibility	77
6. Expanded Grounds for Inquiry: The Pursuit of Intellectually Compelling Ideas	91
Bibliography	111
Index	119

Series Foreword

Educational reform has fallen upon hard times. The traditional assumption that schooling is fundamentally tied to the imperatives of citizenship designed to educate students to exercise civic leadership and public service has been eroded. The schools are now the key institution for producing professional, technically trained, credentialized workers for whom the demands of citizenship are subordinated to the vicissitudes of the marketplace and the commercial public sphere. Given the current corporate and right wing assault on public and higher education, coupled with the emergence of a moral and political climate that has shifted to a new Social Darwinism, the issues which framed the democratic meaning, purpose, and use to which education might aspire have been displaced by more vocational and narrowly ideological considerations.

The war waged against the possibilities of an education wedded to the precepts of a real democracy is not merely ideological. Against the backdrop of reduced funding for public schooling, the call for privatization, vouchers, cultural uniformity, and choice, there are the often ignored larger social realities of material power and oppression. On the national level, there has been a vast resurgence of racism. This is evident in the passing of anti-immigration laws such as Proposition 187 in California, the dismantling of the welfare state, the demonization of black youth that is taking place in the popular media, and the remarkable attention provided by the media to forms of race talk that argue for the intellectual inferiority of blacks or dismiss calls for racial justice as simply a holdover from the "morally bankrupt" legacy of the 1960s.

Poverty is on the rise among children in the United States, with 20 percent of all children under the age of eighteen living below the poverty line. Unemployment is growing at an alarming rate for poor youth of color, especially in the urban centers. While black youth are policed and disciplined in and out of the nation's schools, conservative and liberal educators define education through the ethically limp discourses of privatization, national standards, and global competitiveness.

Many writers in the critical education tradition have attempted to challenge the right wing fundamentalism behind educational and social reform in both the United States and abroad while simultaneously providing ethical signposts for a public discourse about education and democracy that is both prophetic and transformative. Eschewing traditional categories, a diverse number of critical theorists and educators have successfully exposed the political and ethical implications of the cynicism and despair that has become endemic to the discourse of schooling and civic life. In its place, such educators strive to provide a language of hope that inextricably links the struggle over schooling to understanding and transforming our present social and cultural dangers.

At the risk of overgeneralizing, both cultural studies theorists and critical educators have emphasized the importance of understanding theory as the grounded basis for "intervening into contexts and power . . . in order to enable people to act more strategically in ways that may change their context for the better."[1] Moreover, theorists in both fields have argued for the primacy of the political by calling for and struggling to produce critical public spaces, regardless of how fleeting they may be, in which "popular cultural resistance is explored as a form of political resistance."[2] Such writers have analyzed the challenges that teachers will have to face in redefining a new mission for education, one that is linked to honoring the experiences, concerns, and diverse histories and languages that give expression to the multiple narratives that engage and challenge the legacy of democracy.

Equally significant is the insight of recent critical educational work that connects the politics of difference with concrete strategies for addressing the crucial relationships between schooling and the economy, and citizenship and the politics of meaning in communities of multicultural, multiracial, and multilingual schools.

Critical Studies in Education and Culture attempts to address and demonstrate how scholars working in the fields of cultural studies and the critical pedagogy might join together in a radical project and practice informed by theoretically rigorous discourses that affirm the critical but refuse the cynical, and establish hope as central to a critical pedagogical and political practice but eschew a romantic utopianism. Central to such a project is the issue of how pedagogy might provide cultural studies theorists and educators with an opportunity to engage pedagogical practices that are not only transdisciplinary, transgressive, and oppositional, but also connected to a wider project designed to further racial, economic, and political democracy.[3] By taking seriously the relations between culture and power, we further the possibilities of resistance, struggle, and change.

Critical Studies in Education and Culture is committed to publishing work that opens a narrative space that affirms the contextual and the specific while simultaneously recognizing the ways in which such spaces are shot through with issues of power. The series attempts to continue an important legacy of theoretical work in cultural studies in which related debates on pedagogy are understood and addressed within the larger context of social responsibility, civic courage, and the reconstruction of democratic public life. We must keep in mind Raymond Williams's insight that the "deepest impulse (informing cultural politics) is the desire to make learning part of the process of social change itself."[4] Education as a cultural pedagogical practice takes place across multiple sites, which include not only schools and universities but also the mass media, popular culture, and other public spheres, and signals how within diverse contexts, education makes us both subjects of and subject to relations of power.

This series challenges the current return to the primacy of market values and simultaneous retreat from politics so evident in the recent work of educational theorists, legislators, and policy analysts. Professional relegitimation in a troubled time seems to be the order of the day as an increasing number of academics both refuse to recognize public and higher education as critical public spheres and offer little or no resistance to the ongoing vocationalization of schooling, the continuing evisceration of the intellectual labor force, and the current assaults on the working poor, the elderly, and women and children.[5]

Emphasizing the centrality of politics, culture, and power, *Critical Studies in Education and Culture* will deal with pedagogical issues that contribute in imaginative and transformative ways to our understanding of how critical knowledge, democratic values, and social practices can provide a basis for teachers, students, and other cultural workers to redefine their role as engaged and public intellectuals. Each volume will attempt to rethink the relationship between language and experience, pedagogy and human agency, and ethics and social responsibility as part of a larger project for engaging and deepening the prospects of democratic schooling in a multiracial and multicultural society. *Critical Studies in Education and Culture* takes on the responsibility of witnessing and addressing the most pressing problems of public schooling and civic life, and engages culture as a crucial site and strategic force for productive social change.

Henry A. Giroux

NOTES

1. Lawrence Grossberg, "Toward a Genealogy of the State of Cultural Studies," in Cary Nelson and Dilip Parameshwar Gaonkar, eds. *Disciplinarity and Dissent in Cultural Studies* (New York: Routledge, 1996), 143.

2. David Bailey and Stuart Hall, "The Vertigo of Displacement," *Ten 8* 2:3 (1992), 19.

3. My notion of transdisciplinary comes from Mas'ud Zavarzadeh and Donald Morton, "Theory, Pedagogy, Politics: The Crisis of the 'Subject' in the Humanities," in *Theory Pedagogy Politics: Texts for Change*, Mas'ud Zavarzadeh and Donald Morton, eds. (Urbana: University of Illinois Press, 1992), 10. At issue here is neither ignoring the boundaries of discipline-based knowledge nor simply fusing different disciplines, but creating theoretical paradigms, questions, and knowledge that cannot be taken up within the policed boundaries of the existing disciplines.

4. Raymond Williams, "Adult Education and Social Change," in *What I Came to Say* (London: Hutchinson-Radus, 1989), 158.

5. The term "professional legitimation" comes from a personal correspondence with Professor Jeff Williams of East Carolina University.

PUBLISHER'S NOTE: Since its inception in 1985 until his death in May 1997, Paulo Freire was, along with Henry Giroux, the series advisor for the *Critical Studies in Education and Culture*. Throughout his life Paulo Freire maintained a deep commitment to fostering literacy and education as a means by which people might engage in democratic struggles for social and economic justice. His legacy continues in this series.

Preface

This book is the outcome of a number of years of thinking about, reading, and writing on postmodern philosophy. From the time that I was first introduced to postmodern work about a dozen years ago, I sensed that something important and new was being proposed and expressed. The question that I and many others have wrestled with is what that "something" may be. An earlier approach that I took to this question was to interpret postmodern thought as a critique of absolute foundations. I have deemed that interpretation insufficient for reasons that I give in the introduction. However, I would not have made it to the thesis of this book had I not worked through that interpretation. I thank four individuals who commented and critiqued a precursor to this book that took that approach, as members of my dissertation committee: philosophers Jack W. Meiland and Terrence N. Tice, and professors of higher education Lawrence S. Berlin and Robert T. Blackburn, all of the University of Michigan. I also thank professors Ton Beekman, Bill Cave, and Joan Stark for their support.

Postmodern philosophy is often written in an unnecessarily nuanced style. I have endeavored to thoroughly analyze the five philosophers that I cover to reach the core of their ideas, to concisely articulate my interpretations of their work, and to articulate my own ideas in a like manner. Since this book is intended for scholars in all disciplines and fields, I have also avoided the use of philosophical terminology when possible. I expect that some scholars who read this book may take it to be an attack on disciplinary knowledge, or even on modern inquiry generally. Careful readers will not understand that to be my meaning. Based in part on implications that I find in postmodern critique, my aim is to argue that what counts for legitimate intellectual activity in universities and colleges should be expanded, and to develop a foundation for inquiry that would serve as a philosophical basis for such an expansion. Such an ambitious endeavor would require the contributions of many scholars. I hope that this book may serve as a starting point in this direction by stimulating inquiry and debate.

I especially thank my wife and friend, Teresa Herzog Mourad, and our sons, Julian and Theo, for making it possible for me to write this book.

1

Introduction: Modern Inquiry and Postmodern Critique

> We all still need an education in thinking, and first of all, before that, knowledge of what being educated and uneducated in thinking means. In this respect Aristotle gives us a hint in Book IV of his *Metaphysics* (1006a ff.): "For it is uneducated not to have an eye for when it is necessary to look for a proof and when this is not necessary." This sentence demands careful reflection. For it is not yet decided in what way that which needs no proof in order to become accessible to thinking is to be experienced.[1]

This book is about the significance of postmodern critique for what it means to engage in a scholarly inquiry. The philosophers whose work I explore for this purpose are Jean-Francois Lyotard, Michel Foucault, Jacques Derrida, Richard Rorty, and Calvin Schrag. Lyotard's *The Postmodern Condition: A Report on Knowledge* is widely regarded as the most illuminating exposition of postmodern philosophy.[2] Foucault and Derrida are the most influential French postmodern philosophers, and French thought is the most widely influential source of postmodern themes. Rorty is a philosopher of the Anglo-American analytic tradition, who developed a postmodern position on knowledge that signaled his break from that tradition and established him as a leading American postmodern philosopher. He couples his postmodernism with an effort to revive classical American pragmatism, especially the ideas of John Dewey. In contrast, Schrag is an American philosopher who adopts major French postmodern positions and attempts to reconcile them with aspects of modern Continental European philosophy.

The developing idea of postmodernism, or the diverse array of intellectual movements called "postmodern," is still in its infancy. Accordingly, the significance and meaning of postmodernism is the subject of considerable contemporary debate. It is generally agreed, however, that in the last three decades fundamental challenges to modern forms of thought have emerged in many realms of thought and activity. Sometimes more full-blown challenges of this sort are depicted as postmodern. More specifically, among the thinkers primarily to be considered here, postmodernism can be understood in large part as a rejection of what philosopher Jurgen Habermas, who is decidedly not postmodern, calls "the project of modernity" and identifies with the French Enlightenment:

The project of modernity formulated in the eighteenth century by the philosophers of the Enlightenment consisted in their efforts to develop objective science, universal morality and law, and autonomous art according to their inner logic. At the same time, this project intended to release the cognitive potentials of each of their domains from their esoteric forms. The Enlightenment philosophers wanted to utilize this accumulation of specialized culture for the enrichment of everyday life—that is to say, for the rational organization of everyday social life.[3]

These postmodernists claim that this project, which originally challenged the social order and which heavily informs education at all levels in most parts of the world today, has succeeded in becoming dominant as a cultural form yet falls far short of realizing its humane aims. While many contemporary modernists, such as Habermas, agree with this assessment, these postmodernists differ from them in attempting to move intellectual discourse and expression out of the modern, while Habermas and others seek to reform the modern project in some way. These challenges reject belief in the modern idea that intellect can direct human civilization toward a progressive realization of ideal forms of human existence and understanding that are universal, knowable, and achievable through discoveries and applications in such areas as science, civil governance, and aesthetic expression. While, to be sure, not all strands of distinctly modern thought wholly correspond to this widespread belief, and the so-called "project of modernity" is but one version of that belief, it is one that these highly visible and influential postmodernists share in rejecting in every detail. Moreover, it must be admitted that even among some strands of modern thought an explicit critique and opposition directed to some of these details is to be found, quite prominently in some cases. My initial task, however, is not to conflate postmodern with modern critique, but to discern what is distinctive about it.

Today postmodern influence is evident in the sciences, the visual and performing arts, literature, politics, philosophy, religious studies, and cultural studies generally.[4] Since the critiques embedded in postmodern thought radically challenge the status quo in these fields and in higher education generally, and since the university can be understood as the place where such forms of knowledge and expression are now preeminently distinguished and legitimized, it is important to examine the potential significance of postmodern views for inquiry. This study addresses this need by posing questions and expressing positions that provide a direction for scholarly inquiry and debate. By focusing on one major strand of postmodern thought, which is arguably the most readily identifiable and prominent to date, I analyze an intellectual current that is now a subject of intense discussion in many domains within universities and colleges. The fact that the discussion is intense, broad, and sustained suggests that there is something important and distinctive about postmodern thought. In the course of thinking about, reading, and writing on postmodern thought over a number of years, I have proceeded to take and reject several positions on this general question as follows.

One way to distinguish postmodern philosophy is that it criticizes modern social critique on the basis that the latter attempts to ground itself on theory that purports to explain social phenomena in absolute terms or in terms that are tantamount to being absolute. This is a typical interpretation of postmodern thought. For example, forms of postmodern thought termed "poststructural" originate as critiques of one prominent form of "absolute" social explanation, the structuralist social theory identified with the thought of Claude Levi-Strauss. Undoubtedly, many intellectuals in the modern era, in addition to the sophists of ancient Greece, have rejected the idea of an absolute, self-justifying foundation. For this reason, this interpretation of postmodern challenges is insufficient if the aim is to determine what is distinctive about it. Moreover, the idea of an absolute foundation is simply not very relevant to the way that the vast majority of scholars think about and engage in their inquiries. For these reasons, the rejection of absolutes is not a very illuminating way to distinguish postmodern thought.

A second way to distinguish postmodern critique is to approach it as an exploration of the consequences of the rejection of the idea that inquiry can yield a permanent, objective, self-justifying foundation to guide human thought and action. The virtue of this approach is that it suggests that something valuable is being contributed by postmodern thinkers. However, the obvious shortcoming with this interpretation is that it remains wedded to the rejection of absolutism.

A third position is to identify postmodern thought with the idea that knowledge is determined, or at least substantially conditioned, by the social rules that govern discourse and by a general emphasis on the centrality of culture and social relations. While these themes are common among many postmodern thinkers, as well as many modern thinkers, they are not particularly illuminating because they do not get at the core of postmodern thought. They represent some possible consequences of postmodern thought rather than its focal meaning. Postmodern philosophy in particular expresses a distinctive epistemological position, one that cannot, however, be simply reduced to one idea such as the idea that "everything is social," that "everything is cultural," or even that "everything is relative."

A fourth approach, often associated with the charge of radical relativism, is to reject the idea that postmodern thought is a coherent critique of anything at all, but is instead the wholesale leveling of any and all intellectual and moral distinctions, or at least the ones that are basic to most people, including most scholars. Therefore, goes this interpretation, postmodern thought is nihilistic.

The shortcoming with this common interpretation is that it is simply not very thoughtful. It occurs because postmodern thought is just not understood very well by most of its interpreters. This lack of understanding happens for at least two reasons. First, postmodern thought is often highly (and needlessly) nuanced and elliptical, particularly the work of French thinkers (at least in English translation). As a result, it can be very difficult to understand. Second, postmodern work is usually interpreted in modern terms, rather than on its own terms. The common tendency is to carry modern categories and criteria into the reading of postmodern work and to apply those categories in order to understand it. This is the most pervasive problem with most interpretations of postmodern thought. It is understandable in part. Given the difficulty of the texts, and the fact that postmodernists themselves disavow any association with new universalistic truth claims, the idea that postmodern thought has its own terms may seem problematic. However, the result is to largely or even to utterly miss the point.

I believe that the greatest significance of postmodern critique emerges if one examines it in the general context of inquiry. In this context, postmodern thought has important and wide-ranging implications. I interpret postmodern thought as reflecting a fundamental concern for expanding the meaning, possibilities, and purposes of what counts as legitimate scholarly inquiry.

Therefore, I will elaborate what I believe is most distinctive about postmodern thought as it pertains to the philosophical question of inquiry. Since a fundamental concern of higher education is the pursuit of knowledge, and since postmodern philosophers take positions on knowledge that are intended to have broad implications for intellectual and social life generally, an analysis of these positions in the context of inquiry provides a means of eliciting the potential significance of postmodern thought in a way that goes well beyond an exploration of its presence within the confines of a particular discipline. Therefore, in this study the confluence of postmodern thought and the idea of inquiry has a potential significance that goes far beyond any single discipline or field to issues that concern scholars in many areas of inquiry.

Postmodern critique calls into question the efficacy of the assumption that the organized pursuit of knowledge is essentially an endeavor that progresses toward desirable aims that originate in the past. It stakes this position on the claim that basic theoretical deficiencies are apparent in the overall course of inquiry, and that an appropriate response to these deficiencies requires a rethinking of the nature and aims of inquiry. It is especially concerned with encouraging intellect to pursue important ideas besides the idea that reality is composed of things to know. This position, moreover, is not limited to the discipline of philosophy or to any other discipline or field of inquiry. In fact, as I will show, interpreted in the context of inquiry, postmodern critique implies that the very idea of the disciplines, or even more generally, the idea that inquiry must have an established subject or theme that precedes it, is an unduly constraining condition on intellectual capacity. Indeed, postmodern critiques, especially Foucault's and Derrida's, are not only about an alternative idea of inquiry; they are also exercises of it.

This interpretation helps to explain the largely misunderstood postmodern rejection of modern progress. Postmodernists do not reject the idea that social conditions can be vastly improved or the idea that intellectuals can and should play a very important role in making life better through social change. Foucault is a good example of a postmodern philosopher who rejected modern social critique and who was very active in organized social and political protests in the 1960s and 1970s.

What postmodern philosophers reject is the idea that desirable social change is conceptualized and pursued as social progress in the modern sense. "Modern progress" is the idea that forms of human knowledge, social organization, and creative expression are progressively improved over time, either gradually or through successive waves of intellectual revolutions. This idea is wedded to the pursuit of knowledge for its own sake, by which I mean simply the idea that knowledge is pursued for love for learning.[5] This idea is wedded to modern progress by the belief that if academic freedom is maintained and supported by society, and if scholars and higher education institutions retain a significant degree of professional and institutional autonomy, then free inquiry will make major contributions toward the betterment of the "human condition" generally. Even though many scholars may disavow absolutes, they retain belief in the idea that their particular endeavors are part of a larger, inexorable story called modern progress.

For postmodern philosophers, then, the idea of making life better, and the idea that intellectual inquiry is a means toward doing so, are important aims. However, they claim that modern proposals for making life better unwisely attempt to justify themselves on the basis that they capture ways of thinking and living that are, or come close to, the nature of things, including human nature.

To understand postmodern critique in the context of inquiry, one must first examine the modern aims of inquiry, at least as they are commonly regarded. What, then, are the modern foundations of inquiry in universities and colleges? In what ways are they linked to the idea of progress? I answer these questions in Chapter 2 by examining the ideas of four established thinkers and institutional leaders of the twentieth century who present currently typical visions of the intrinsic worth of higher learning. They are Robert Maynard Hutchins, Alfred North Whitehead, A. Bartlett Giamatti, and Jaroslav Pelikan.[6] I show how each of these thinkers grounds the pursuit of knowledge for its own sake on an aim pronounced in the past, and how this value is ultimately dependent on the inquiry's adherence to overarching aims initially established in previous eras. I also indicate that each of the individuals whose work I examine here emphasize the value of inquiry as an active engagement or experience. However, the intrinsic value of inquiry is rooted in the past, in that the past establishes the overriding aims of inquiry.

In Chapters 3 and 4, I analyze how the postmodern critique of this modern formula is articulated by Lyotard, Rorty, Schrag, Foucault, and Derrida, respectively. First, I show how each philosopher critiques the modern foundations of inquiry and its association with progress. Second and most importantly, I show that the work of each philosopher implies an idea of inquiry that emphasizes intellectual activity and experience over the discovery and production of knowledge. Most importantly, I show how these critiques provide the basis for a viable and robust alternative to conventional ideas of inquiry. I elicit the most important elements of these critiques that can serve as the raw material that I will use to develop an alternative concept of inquiry.

The fact that each of the critiques is fundamental suggests that they are responding to a basic condition of inquiry as it is currently comprehended and practiced by scholars. Further, the basic condition that they are responding to acts as a significant constraint on intellect and it has something to do with the past. The question that my analysis of the five postmodernists leaves, then, is what the basic condition is, and how does it act as an undesirable constraint on intellect.

To develop an alternative idea of inquiry in more depth, then, it is important to think about what it means to engage in a conventional or modern inquiry generally. Postmodern philosophers, along with some modern philosophers, allege that the pursuit of an essential epistemological foundation remains a basic aim of modern philosophical work. Rorty, for example, asserts that "analytic philosophy is still committed to the construction of a permanent, neutral framework for inquiry, and thus for all of culture."[7] Richard Bernstein uses the term "objectivism" to signify "the basic conviction that there is or must be some permanent, ahistorical matrix or framework to which we can ultimately appeal in determining the nature of rationality, knowledge, truth, reality, goodness, or rightness."[8] Hilary Putnam, in distinguishing his own position from Bernard Williams's view that contemporary physics provides "at least a sketch of an 'absolute conception of the world,'" states that "many analytic philosophers today subscribe to such a view, and for a philosopher who subscribes to it the task of philosophy becomes largely one of commenting on and speculating about the progress of science, especially as it bears or seems to bear on the various traditional problems of philosophy."[9]

The special status of the theoretical pursuit of knowledge of objective reality and of the idea that particular pursuits are contributions to a comprehensive knowledge of reality are dependent on a number of epistemological assumptions that have been the subject of intense philosophical debate, particularly since David Hume's critique of objective knowledge of reality in the eighteenth century. Beginning with Immanuel Kant toward the end of that century, philosophers have attempted to overcome, or at least, to qualify Hume's critique by advancing theories of knowledge that, if they do not accord it strict objectivity, refer to objective knowledge in the extended sense indicated in the accounts of it given in Rorty's and Bernstein's critiques, namely, the idea of a permanent, ahistorical foundation that can be relied on as an essential condition for knowledge.

However, there is no knowledge, and thus no theory of knowledge, without an inquiry. Although a fundamental value of inquiry is to not accept truth assertions without subjecting them to critical analysis within disciplines and fields of inquiry, the foundations of inquiry that serve as a general guide for inquiry across disciplines and fields are rarely examined or even acknowledged. The sheer magnitude of knowledge and the splintering of inquiry into highly specialized lines contributes to this situation because it makes scholars become immersed in the particular domains of knowledge that exists before them. Yet the existence of this foundation, or what I refer to as the basic condition of inquiry, and its limitations is inherent in the very fabric of modern scholarly inquiry and in the structure of higher education.

In Chapter 5, I argue that this basic condition of inquiry in relation to the past is the belief that the essential foundation of inquiry in the university is pursuit of knowledge of phenomena that are assumed to (1) exist before and independent of inquiry, and (2) persist essentially unchanged by inquiry. Other basic purposes of higher education are obvious. However, fulfillment of these other purposes is dependent on there being knowledge of preexistent reality to transmit and apply. Further, inquiry that seeks knowledge of preexistent reality with the aim of showing that it should be changed does not avoid this critique.

I argue that the disciplines are the core manifestation of this foundation. In effect, the disciplines are this preexisting reality. I want to stress that my claim that pursuit of preexisting, persistent reality is the essential foundation of inquiry also holds with regard to applied and professional fields as well as the basic disciplines, even though the latter are the core embodiment of it. Like the disciplines, they are "subjects" of inquiry that are assumed to have an essentially stable and permanent existence. Most importantly, I argue that the essential stature of this modern foundation is an undesirable constraint on the capacity of intellect. This foundation unduly limits the capacity of intellectuals to make better worlds. It is the basis upon which the intellectual community inadvertently constricts the scope of its activities.

Although interdisciplinary inquiry is largely an extension of the disciplines, the concept of cross-disciplinarity provides initial direction for an alternative, more flexible foundation. The existence and growth of cross-disciplinary inquiry can be interpreted to imply that there exists a growing desire among many scholars to conceive knowledge and inquiry in new ways. This desire can be understood as two basic themes underlying cross-disciplinarity that together can be used as a guide for an alternative foundation. First, it suggests an idea of inquiry in which an inquirer essentially constructs a particular ground in the course of inquiry in ways that do not require adherence to a prevailing disciplinary or an interdisciplinary approach. Second, cross-disciplinarity suggests a desire to traverse this boundary, preexistent reality, and the disciplines as this boundary's collective manifestation altogether.

The problem that Chapter 5 leaves for development is that an alternative idea of inquiry must be based on a philosophical foundation that goes beyond the pursuit of preexisting reality, yet is capable of sustaining the latter in a form that does not have an unduly constraining effect on intellect. If it did not sustain inquiry of preexisting reality, it would imply that 2600 years of inquiry of preexisting, persisting reality is not legitimate, which is unreasonable. Thus, the alternative foundation must be useful in the sense of being a reasonable basis for expanding what counts as legitimate inquiry beyond the pursuit of preexisting reality, rather than a foundation that substitutes a new constraint for an old one.

In Chapter 6, I develop this alternative foundation based on the ideas obtained from my interpretations of the five postmodern philosophers and on my analysis of cross-disciplinarity. To resituate modern inquiry within a broader context, I focus on the idea of inquiry as an intellectual experience. The focus is to emphasize inquiry as an intellectual activity that is inquirer-centered rather than object- or knowledge-centered. The key concept that I introduce is the experience of "intellectually compelling ideas." Disciplinary pursuits of knowledge become variations of a particular way of expressing one intellectually compelling idea, namely the idea of reality, as independent of the inquirer and accessible to intellect. Under the alternative foundation that I propose, the idea of pursuing preexisting reality remains, but it no longer bears the nature or effect of an unduly constraining foundation. Most importantly, the conception of intellectually compelling ideas justifies the creation of an intellectual space outside the disciplines and applied fields that makes possible forms of inquiry that are not limited by the pursuit of knowledge of preexistent reality. Outside the disciplines, the aim of inquiry is to explore rather than to explain, to create rather than to improve. It produces "postdisciplinary" forms of knowledge that are outside explanations of preexistent reality. In this space, one views received ideas as tools or premises to be used to generate intellectually compelling ideas of what reality *can* become.

A university that is postmodern, then, would be a place that is focused on expanding the idea of scholarly practice, such that inquiry that seeks to accurately explain preexistent reality becomes only one form of inquiry, rather than the fundamental form. For postdisciplinary kinds of intellectual activities to occur, postdisciplinary inquiry would need to be independent of existing disciplines and fields. I propose such a research structure, which I call "postdisciplinary research programs." These programs would utilize groups of scholars from disparate (rather than complementary) disciplines to explore the ways that existing concepts, theories, models, facts, methods, and assumptions, and parts thereof, could be rearranged to generate compelling new lines of inquiry. I conclude this book with a short description of the basis for intellectual community in a postmodern university and for its relation to other communities.

NOTES

1. Martin Heidegger, "The End of Philosophy and the Task of Thinking," in *Basic Writings*, ed. David Farrell Krell (New York: Harper & Row, 1977), 392.

2. Jean-Francois Lyotard, *The Postmodern Condition: A Report on Knowledge*, trans. Geoffrey Bennington and Brian Massumi (Minneapolis: University of Minnesota Press, 1984).

3. Jurgen Habermas, "Modernity—An Incomplete Project," in *The Anti-Aesthetic: Essays on Postmodern Culture*, ed. Hal Foster (Port Townsend, Wash.: Bay Press, 1983), 9.

4. Good detailed expositions of various aspects of postmodernism include Steven Best and Douglas Kellner, *Postmodern Theory: Critical Interrogations* (New York: Guilford, 1991); Jonathan Culler, *On Deconstruction: Theory and Criticism After Structuralism* (Ithaca: Cornell University, 1982); Foster, *Anti-Aesthetic*; and David Harvey, *The Condition of Postmodernity* (London: Blackwell, 1989).

5. The classic expression of the idea that the pursuit of knowledge is for its own sake is from Aristotle: "the wise man, even when by himself, can contemplate truth, and the better the wiser he is. . . . And this activity alone would seem to be loved for its own sake; for nothing arises from it apart from the contemplating, while from practical activities we gain more or less apart from the action . . . the activity of intellect, which is contemplative, seems both to be superior in worth and to aim at no end beyond itself." *Nicomachean Ethics*, trans. W. D. Ross, rev. J. Barnes (Oxford: Oxford University Press, 1984), Book X.7, 1177a–1177b20.

6. It is perhaps no accident that among these individuals only Whitehead is a philosopher, and even then more typical than influential in this regard. No twentieth-century philosopher appears to have had any marked influence on the articulation or enactment of these foundations apart from compliance to them.

7. Richard Rorty, *Philosophy and the Mirror of Nature* (Princeton: Princeton University Press, 1979), 8.

8. Richard J. Bernstein, *Beyond Objectivism and Relativism: Science, Hermeneutics, and Praxis* (Philadelphia: University of Pennsylvania Press, 1983), 8.

9. Hilary Putnam, *Renewing Philosophy* (Cambridge, Mass.: Harvard University Press, 1992), 2.

2

The Modern Foundations of Progress in the Pursuit of Knowledge

In this chapter, I examine the work of four eminent higher education leaders and scholars as it associates inquiry with progress toward the four larger purposes or aims of truth, science, democracy, and humanity. In turn, each of these aims is claimed to be associated with the social good. I take these aims to be readily recognizable and valued by many, probably most, scholars, though they do not exhaust the aims of higher education. Further, I will assume that many scholars believe, at least tacitly, that inquiry "for its own sake" has a larger meaning grounded in a close relation with one or more of these purposes.

The writers examined here locate the origin of each of these four aims with particularly important periods in Western intellectual history, including classical Greece, the Renaissance, and the Enlightenment. Modern inquiry is construed to be a collective enterprise that, over time, progresses toward an increasingly better realization of these fundamental aims. I show how each thinker critiques current practice in higher education and advocates a particular idea of inquiry as a collective enterprise that is claimed to advance the larger aim and, thereby, the good of society as a whole. Each of them proposes a unified enterprise and a unified society.

In addition, each of the individuals whose work I examine here emphasizes the value of inquiry as an active engagement or experience. However, the intrinsic value of inquiry is rooted in the past, in that a pronouncement on the nature and purposes of inquiry made in the past serves as foundations for contemporary inquiry. It is significant that these foundations are largely unquestioned by scholars, even though their meaning has always been a source of contention.

My treatment of these aims separately is not intended to suggest that they are mutually exclusive or that they do not imply each other. For example, it will be apparent that the aim of truth is implicit in each of the other aims as they are presented by the writers examined here.

TRUTH

> We cannot talk about the intellectual powers of men . . . unless our philosophy in general tells us that there is knowledge and that there is a difference between true and false.[1]

For Robert Maynard Hutchins, influential educator, lawyer, and president and chancellor of the University of Chicago from 1929 to 1950, the aim of inquiry is truth. Hutchins follows a classical definition of truth: "Theoretical truth tells us what is the case: practical truth tells us what should be done."[2] The pursuit of knowledge is justified on the basis that it progresses toward a more complete knowledge of truth.

In his key work, *The Higher Learning in America*, Hutchins specifies two essential, complementary means of developing the human intellect.[3] First, every inquirer must have an education that draws out human nature.[4] These elements are intellectual virtues, or good intellectual habits, which Hutchins specifies according to Aquinas's formulation, itself derived from Aristotle.[5] There are three speculative virtues: the habit of induction; scientific knowledge or the habit of demonstration; and philosophical wisdom, which is "scientific knowledge, combined with intuitive reason, of things highest by nature, first principles and first causes."[6] There are two practical virtues: art, which is the capacity to make according to reason, and prudence, or right reason as the basis for action.[7] A general liberal arts curriculum that emphasizes the study of Great Books, which are "those books which have through the centuries attained the dimensions of classics," meets this requirement.[8] It is important to emphasize that Hutchins believed this curriculum is crucial not only because it provides students with a common stock of fundamental ideas; he also emphasized the significance of a general curriculum for unifying scholars engaged in the pursuit of knowledge.[9]

The second requirement for the development of human intellect is the ability to engage in independent intellectual work in order to know a part of the order of reality in great depth.[10] However, if intellectual pursuit is left to pursue its own particular ends, it results in "complete and thoroughgoing disorder."[11] Since the foundation of the university is the pursuit of truth, inquiry can progress only if it is organized according to the true nature of reality. The inherent structure of truth is the basis for this organization.[12] The foundation is metaphysics, or the study of first principles as Aristotle conceived it. For Hutchins, since the aim of higher education is wisdom, and since wisdom is knowledge of principles and causes, then metaphysics is the highest wisdom.[13] Upon this ground of absolute truth, the rest of inquiry and knowledge is organized.[14]

In subsequent works, Hutchins attempted to demonstrate that this classical understanding of inquiry is relevant to contemporary concerns. In so doing, the connection between the pursuit of truth and progress is developed. In *Education for Freedom*, it is acknowledged that higher learning must address basic political and social questions of the present.[15] However, contemporary problems are not unique to the twentieth century. Instead, they are particular manifestations of problems that are inherent to human existence and they should be approached that way. "What is the basis of these principles of law, equality, and justice? In the first place, in order to believe in these principles at all we must believe that there is such a thing as truth and that in these matters we can discover it."[16]

The problem is that in universities, "We have been concerned with the transitory and superficial instead of the enduring and basic problems of life and of society."[17] "When men begin to doubt whether there is such a thing as truth or whether it can ever be discovered, the search for truth must lose that precision which it had in the minds of those who founded the American universities. . . . The universities, instead of leading us through the chaos of the modern world, mirror its confusion."[18] If universities do not approach contemporary problems properly, it is because they are not united on a foundation of fundamental truths, since those truths are the only basis by which real-life problems can be properly overcome.

In *The Conflict of Education*, Hutchins continues to advocate this position as the means of overcoming a pervasive cultural crisis: "If there is to be a new cultural epoch and not simply a further cultural collapse, the distinguishing feature of the new epoch must be this: it must combine discovery and discussion. The object must be, while retaining and encouraging the drive toward discovery, to restore the conditions of conversation."[19]

In *Conflict*, Hutchins explicitly acknowledges the need for scholarly debate. However, the basis for reform remains the unified pursuit of the organic whole of knowledge. If the university is to function according to its nature as epitomized by the Greek academy and by the medieval university, it must provide a common background of learning.[20] This common background of learning, a true liberal education, affords everyone access to the Great Conversation, or the Western heritage of great ideas.[21]

In *Great Books: The Foundation of a Liberal Education*, Hutchins reaffirms his classical idea of inquiry.[22] The true inquirer

seeks to clarify the basic problems and to understand the way in which one problem bears upon another . . . for example, the relation between the immortality of the soul and the problem of the best form of government. . . . The liberally educated man understands, by understanding the distinctions and interrelations of the basic fields of subject matter, the differences and connections between poetry and history, science and philosophy, theoretical and practical science. . . . The liberally educated man has a mind that can operate well in all fields.[23]

While the Conversation includes great scientific works, Hutchins also states that they do not establish the parameters of truth.[24] Further, the Conversation is ubiquitous. Even the question of whether there is truth is a part of the Conversation. Skepticism represents one point of view within it.[25] In *The University of Utopia*, Hutchins refines further the nature of this Conversation and what it means for the idea that knowledge progresses.[26] While "education is a conversation aimed at truth," the aim of the University "is to work toward a definition of real points of agreement and disagreement . . . not in the hope of obtaining unanimity, but in the hope of obtaining clarity. The object is not agreement but communication."[27]

Although the existence of truth is retained, Hutchins expresses here an emphasis on diversity of views and mutual comprehension rather than agreement regarding the truth. Further, an emphasis of the Great Conversation is participation in the experience of inquiry. The maintenance of the Conversation is crucial, rather than coming to answers that would narrow it or even bring it to an end. Moreover, such a community, if realized, would have success "dealing with the kind of practical issues that seem beyond resolution in the West today."[28] The Great Conversation is progressive and practical.

In *The Learning Society*, Hutchins applies the pursuit of truth to transformative social change.[29] The purpose of inquiry is not simply to contribute to a common inheritance of knowledge. In addition, it must civilize the world: "A world community learning to be civilized, learning to be human, is at last a possibility. . . . Whether it does or not depends on the transformation of values. . . . A society in which everybody has a liberal education . . . is one in which values may be transformed."[30] On appearance, the emphasis of the classical position seems to have changed from the pursuit of truth to a critical questioning of contemporary social values. Yet, recognition of the need for inquiry to address current issues does not mean that the nature of the Conversation is itself altered. The Great Conversation is capable of absorbing new issues. The pursuit of knowledge remains an active engagement of intellect with Great Ideas. The authority of the past is still the guide for the thoughtful resolution of current problems, because, in essence, current problems are essentially particular manifestations of classical questions. Therefore, the appropriate inquiry for these problems leads intellect toward truth. The basic questions, principal modes of reasoned inquiry, and solutions concerning the human condition are enduring and universal in character. The accumulated wisdom of the Conversation establishes the terms and conditions of inquiry and debate.

SCIENCE

> The present contains all that there is. It is holy ground; but only because the present is the past, and it is the future.[31]

In *The Function of Reason*, British philosopher and mathematician Alfred North Whitehead (1861–1947) develops a contrast between two notions of the concept of reason that corresponds to Hutchins's traditional distinction between theoretical and practical knowledge. However, Whitehead's analysis of reason leads him to a different understanding of the pursuit of knowledge and a different foundation to justify the pursuit. For Whitehead, inquiry aims for knowledge of an objective, systematically ordered reality that is grounded on, though not limited to, scientific knowledge.[32] Unlike Hutchins, for Whitehead the idea of progress is not construed within a classical framework. Whitehead introduces an explicit requirement that important knowledge must be useful. Further, wisdom does not simply consist in knowing truth. Most importantly, it is an ability to use knowledge to add value to experience.[33] Inquiry aims to apply general principles to particular experience in order to transform immediate experience and thereby to add value to life.[34] Reality is historical and subject to change. However, it remains orderly, objective, absolute, and theoretically accessible.

In *Reason*, Whitehead delineates two aspects of Reason, which he calls speculative and practical.[35] Both aspects figure in the pursuit of knowledge. Speculative Reason seeks a complete understanding of reality, whereas practical Reason, seeks an immediate method of action.[36] Speculative Reason "is driven forward by the ultimate faith that all particular fact is understandable as illustrating the general principles of its own nature and of its status among other particular facts."[37] "Science has been developed under the impulse of the speculative Reason, the desire for explanatory knowledge."[38]

Practical Reason is subordinate to speculative Reason, but it too is necessary for progress: "In this function Reason is the practical embodiment of the urge to transform mere existence into the good existence, and to transform the good existence into the better existence."[39] However, considered alone, it provides no purpose.[40] For Whitehead, science is an instance of the practical aspect of Reason. Alone, it gives the knower no guidance on decisions pertaining to the determination of *proper* ends, and it can be destructive: "Some of the major disasters of mankind have been produced by the narrowness of men with a good methodology."[41] Scientific method, being an instance of practical Reason, is heir to primitive forms of life. Method is the means of survival.[42]

In contrast, speculative Reason is uniquely human.[43] However, it too has a decadent quality. Absent method, it can be "anarchic," because alone it is "the flight after the unattainable."[44] For Whitehead, human civilization improves itself over time because it has to, and practical Reason, which renders knowledge effective, is essential in that improvement. Speculation that is productive is verified as such by practical Reason, because practical Reason confirms thought that is capable of being fact. "The basis of all authority is the supremacy of fact over thought."[45] Inquiry embodies the advancement of civilization by the capacity to utilize an interplay of both aspects of Reason in process.

A key element of progress is technological advance. It is made possible because "speculative and practical Reason have at last made contact."[46] However, according to Whitehead, human history has been plagued by "the refusal to speculate freely."[47] In modernity, the obscurantists are scientists.[48] The modern problem is scientific dogmatism that restrains an "understanding of the proper functions of speculative thought" in the progress of civilization. There is a "natural human tendency to turn a successful methodology into a dogmatic creed."[49]

"In scientific training, the first thing to do with an idea is to prove it. But . . . In our first contact with a set of propositions, we commence by appreciating their importance. . . . We do not attempt, in the strict sense, to prove or to disprove anything unless its importance makes it worthy of that honour."[50] Thus, scientific method is not an end in itself. The importance of an idea is determined according to its use.[51] However, false propositions are not likely to be useful. "By utilising an idea, I mean relating it to that stream, compounded of sense perceptions, feelings, hopes, desires, and of mental activities adjusting thought to thought, which forms our life."[52] By use, then, Whitehead means that ideas are to be related to experience, which is broadly construed to include all mental activity. Use can include, but does not demand, the application of knowledge toward the accomplishment of some material end. The essence of utilization is intellectual. However, it must be relevant to action to be productive.[53]

Thus, the advancement of civilization is a function of the advancement of intellect. What are ends proper to the advancement of civilization, and thus, proper to higher education?

Animals have progressively undertaken the task of adapting the environment to themselves. . . . In the case of mankind this active attack on the environment is the most prominent fact in his existence . . . the explanation of this active attack on the environment is a three-fold urge: (i) to live, (ii) to live well, (iii) to live better.[54]

The advancement of civilization means, in some collective measure, an increase in satisfaction. Collective satisfaction is accomplished by the application of knowledge to alter the environment, or "a practical technique for well-attested ends."[55]

Education is the guidance of the individual towards a comprehension of the art of life; and by the art of life I mean the most complete achievement of varied activity expressing the potentialities of that living creature in the face of its actual environment.[56]

The simple accumulation of facts is itself not artful and is, therefore, not educative. Inquiry must cultivate the foresight and ability to actively use ideas to create oneself in the world. Wisdom is the selection and use of knowledge to add value to experience. The pursuit of knowledge is, therefore, an ongoing expression and realization of one's intellectual potential.[57] Progress issues from within individual mind.[58] A disciplined mind seeks to realize possibilities that enlarge the satisfaction of one's life. Above all, inquiry is valuable as an experience of purposive intellectual engagement with ideas.[59]

To accomplish these aims, the curriculum must be connected. "The solution which I am urging, is to eradicate the fatal disconnection of subjects which kills the vitality of our modern curriculum. There is only one subject matter for education, and that is Life in all its manifestations . . . this single unity.[60] "The life of man is founded on Technology, Science, Art and Religion. All four are interconnected and issue from his total mentality."[61] Universities should inculcate the habit of understanding the world in terms of principles rather than details.[62]

Contra Hutchins, study of the classics is not the basis of imaginative thought. The popularity of the classics in medieval universities is not explained by attributing to these texts the quality of intrinsic greatness. Rather, "there was a large demand for classical scholars for the mere purposes of tuition; there was a classical tone in all learned walks of life, so that aptitude for classics was a synonym for ability."[63]

Thus, for Whitehead, the classics are not the measure of virtue because a classical inquiry does not yield ideas that are likely to add value to human experience. The classics cannot teach moderns how to live. Instead, they have historical value. They are important because there is no substitute for first-hand knowledge.[64] Historical knowledge is valuable if it is useful.[65] Contemplation for its own sake "carries with it the decadence of civilization."[66] Inquiry, properly construed, is not removed from action.[67] Specialization is essential because for one to be a true inquirer, "mankind is naturally specialist."[68]

Whitehead's faith, that modernity means the progress of knowledge, is firmly rooted on a foundation of science and its methods, and aims high for knowledge of the heavens. Although Whitehead rejects the position that science alone shows people how to live, he affirms that scientific method is the basis for distinguishing between idle and productive speculative Reason. Scientific verification confirms ideas that are fact, and productive ideas can only be utilized for desired ends if they are based on fact. Scientific method is, then, the ground for speculative reasons that aim to change one's world.

DEMOCRACY

> I use the word civility often. The word is important to my view of the University as a place . . . where the larger goal of intellectual training is a civic one—the making not only of future scholars but of good citizens.[69]

For the late A. Bartlett Giamatti, Renaissance scholar and president of Yale University from 1978 to 1986, the aim of the pursuit of knowledge is the creation of a democratic citizenry. In collections of his essays published as *The University and the Public Interest* and *A Free and Ordered Space: The Real World of the University*, he argues that if one pursues knowledge properly, then one learns how to be a good citizen, because the principles of the pursuit of knowledge are also the basis for good citizenship. These principles are freedom and order in their proper relation, and they are principles of democracy: "by the pursuit of learning for its own sake . . . the mind and spirit are toughened and made capacious in the habits and conditions of freedom." [70]

The university's values are encapsulated in "the capacity of individuals to associate in a spirit of free inquiry," and these values are "free, rational and humane investigation and behavior."[71] Political freedom, according to Giamatti, is freedom of "belief, speech and choice."[72] By coming to know the meaning and values of free inquiry, a person comes to know the meaning and value of political freedom. If one is committed to these values, one knows what it means to live as a part of a democratic political community and how to be a good citizen.

Although Giamatti asserts that both the university and society have significantly to do with freedom and democracy, he also states that there is an important difference between them. The difference is that the formal power structure of the university is a hierarchy, rather than a balance of powers. Giamatti claims, however, that this hierarchy is not authoritarian because it acts democratically in advancing its essential purpose. Executive leadership is collaborative for the purpose of promoting "the educational process, in which the individual, often alone, often with others, seeks constantly to clarify limits in order to surpass them, constantly seeks to order the mind so as to set it free. That seeking is the University's essence."[73]

Hutchins had claimed that the intrinsic aim of the pursuit of knowledge for its own sake is to discover and live according to the truth. In this way, one realizes freedom. Yet, according to Hutchins, truth, not freedom, is the real object of inquiry. In contrast, for Giamatti, the pursuit of knowledge has intrinsic value primarily because intellectual imagination is the essence of humanity and that, in turn, is freely expressed in the pursuit of knowledge. "The University is the guardian of the imagination that both defines and asserts our humanity . . . the foe of the merely random, insistent on order while urging freedom, convinced that the human mind, out of nature, can fashion shapes and patterns nature never bore."[74]

For Giamatti, a Renaissance scholar, language reveals the truth, which is both multiple and whole.[75] "As individuals and as a people we define through language what we have, and what we will be. . . . Without a respect for its awesome power we can never find out who we are, and thus never . . . become citizens."[76] Knowledge of scientific principles of inquiry is an integral element of this idea of progress, not because it produces scientific knowledge but because these principles are "various languages that science speaks" and are imaginative in character.[77] Science and the arts are unified upon "the reality of language."[78] Expressive of multiple perspectives, language also connects those perspectives and connects human beings with each other. Language must be respected as the means of intellectual imagination and the possibility of democracy. Language has this connective function only if humans come to understand language through a liberal education.

For Giamatti, the heart of inquiry is the humanities, because language is their central concern. His exemplary model is the Renaissance and classical origins of the *studia humanitatis*.[79] To be educated according to the Western tradition of the humanities frees the mind to create meaning based on the past. Order and continuity of thought are ensured by a common, disciplined approach to thinking.[80] Further, solo contemplation is not a proper use of language unless its end is "the larger or common good, the freedom that the individual mind wishes for itself, it seeks for others."[81] Humanism is "celebrated active engagement with the world, not contemplative repose. The purpose of study was to improve the political life of the community."[82]

A humanities education embodies a respect for the original meanings of words and their history.[83] To understand language, to know how to be a free citizen, one must understand language historically, according to a tradition, because "language is the bearer of tradition . . . words give first principles and last things."[84] This tradition is "our common Western heritage," and a liberal education, properly construed, "is one of the central means whereby that heritage is made continuous and available to the future."[85] The progress of inquiry toward greater knowledge of the whole is progress toward greater democracy. Although interpretation is often multiple and dynamic, multiple meanings are connected because they are grounded in a unified, common language, the language of the Western tradition. "It is the tradition of seeing from various vantage points, the principle of perspective and hence of multiple perspectives, that the humanities want to keep alive and well."[86]

Inquiry is an active experience with the enduring values of the past through the common language of the Western intellectual tradition. The inquirer knows how to find objective meaning in this tradition in order to create a coherent future. The apparent flux of experience is reconstituted in accord with the language of the West to make history.[87] The need for connections rooted in the Western tradition justifies a common core curriculum.[88]

[T]here is no specialization in a democracy unless there is first a broad, deep base of shared assumptions and perceptions, growing out of a carefully wrought curriculum, about where we have come from and what that pluralism of values and backgrounds and peoples had as a purpose, and how important is the unity in and through that diversity.[89]

The connections need not be logical; the overriding need is that they are true to the Western tradition, even if they are contradictory. Giamatti simply rejects the idea that paradoxes are problems and that they belie his claim that the Western heritage is unified. Paradoxes in that heritage are objective limits that humans cannot explain and must respect.[90]

Inquiry should "follow the mind, not restrain it."[91] Therefore, academic departments should function as "forces in a field rather than feudal baronies," and should reflect "the mutual dependence and reliance of the various parts," including the fine and performing arts.[92] Freely inquiring minds should "seek to see the truth from as many vantage points as humankind can summon," and should have a "healthy disregard of boundaries—where they only impede the pursuit of learning."[93]

According to Giamatti, this fluidity of knowledge is insulated from causing fragmentation of thought and belief within and across minds by comprehension of the connection between order and freedom, "that essential, grand connection."

> The order necessary to keep that freedom from collapsing into merely competitive appetites or colliding gusts of anarchy is, first, in this country, a respect for law and the processes of law. But it is more than an order external; it is the internalized order that grows with self-government, self-civilizing.[94]

For Hutchins and Whitehead, the object of the pursuit of knowledge is the nature of reality, and it is known philosophically and scientifically. For Giamatti, the object of knowledge is Western culture, and it is known through the experience of its languages. For Giamatti, the pursuit of knowledge for its own sake in the university, and freedom of speech and belief in the polis, insure democracy, the political order of true citizens. The substance of good citizenship is knowledge of the common language of the Western cultural and intellectual tradition. Knowledge of that language is the guide for how to be a good citizen who contributes to the common good. Belief in these connections holds Giamatti's vision of free inquiry and progress together. The multiplicity of interpretations is possible only on the basis of a common language, the dominant Western heritage.

HUMANITY

> "Knowledge its own end," then, is a first principle for the university that must not only be reaffirmed but must be applied more thoroughly than ever.[95]

Historian Jaroslav Pelikan's *The Idea of the University: A Reexamination* is a recent critique of John Henry Newman's statement of the aims of higher education, *The Idea of a University*.[96] These lectures by Newman in 1852 provide the classic modern-era justification of the idea that the pursuit of knowledge is for its own sake. Pelikan's analysis of Newman is also a summation of the thought of Hutchins, Whitehead, and Giamatti that both preserves and extends their ideas. In the course of updating Newman's position, Pelikan attempts to link truth, science, and democracy to a social mission that extends the reach of inquiry to the global community, particularly "third world" societies. For Pelikan, progress in knowledge requires that inquiry advance the welfare of humanity world-wide.

Like Newman, Hutchins, Whitehead, and Giamatti, knowledge its own end is for Pelikan the "first principle" of the university, but for Pelikan the meaning of this idea must be broadened to be justified as progressive.[97] Like Hutchins, for Pelikan first principles ground the pursuit of any inquiry because "they are always present whether they be recognized or not."[98] Further, Pelikan emphasizes the idea of intellectual virtues. However, he does not equate them with well-developed intellectual habits in the pursuit of knowledge. Rather, intellectual virtues are ethical values that govern inquiry.[99] In common with Whitehead and Giamatti, Pelikan asserts that while one's creative solitude must be respected and provided for, the inquirer should not merely contemplate for itself; there must be communication with others.[100] Most importantly, whereas Hutchins believes that knowing the hierarchy of truths in their proper order is the basis of inquiry, for Pelikan trust in rationality must be predicated on "a deepening appreciation for other ways of knowing and thinking" in addition to prevailing Western intellectual traditions.[101]

This openness to ideas that are not grounded in predominant traditions in Western philosophy, science, or culture makes it possible for Pelikan to link progress with a commitment to the global community. A point of emphasis for Pelikan is the pursuit of knowledge for fundamental social change across national boundaries. He is careful to specify that "critical understanding, not adherence or discipleship, whether uncritical or critical, is the criterion."[102] He argues that a scientific formation of mind and critical intelligence are necessary for progressive social change.[103]

In contrast to Giamatti's focus on the production of individual citizens within a democracy, Pelikan broadens the concept of citizenship. There is a distinct moral contract between the university, as a center of well-educated people who discover and transmit knowledge, and local, national, and international communities, especially the Third World.[104] This duty is based on the fact that the university is the principal community where higher rationality examines all communities.[105] Further, there is an "urgency to review the international context of the university curriculum . . . with a view to identifying the university's duties" to the world community.[106]

Moreover, Pelikan argues that the integrity of the university as a community that pursues knowledge "lies to a considerable extent in the development of mechanisms" for collaborative inquiry that goes beyond not only disciplinary and campus boundaries but also "across national boundaries and across continents."[107] While quoting Giamatti favorably regarding the need to affirm both freedom and order, Pelikan argues that scholars need to "affirm old ways of being both free and responsible, and to learn new ways of doing so," in order for knowledge for inquiry to progress.[108]

A related consideration regarding the curriculum that is of particular concern to Pelikan is the need for the pursuit of knowledge to be connected with practical, real-world problems.[109] Like Hutchins and Giamatti, he takes a hard look at the entrenchment of academic departments. Pelikan suggests the possibility of cross-disciplinary integration, including the integration of arts and sciences areas with professional schools that share common subject matter, based on the need to apply critical philosophical reflection to practice.[110] Like Whitehead, practical Reason for Pelikan has a key role relative to speculative Reason. Quoting Whitehead favorably, Pelikan states that the justification of the university "necessarily implies the movement of questions and ideas in both directions."[111] He argues that "knowledge its own end" implies that teaching and scholarship go hand-in-hand.[112]

Pelikan's effort to show that Newman's basic idea of a university is an educationally justifiable foundation by extending its reach seems to go too smoothly, given Pelikan's acknowledgment that the "university is in crisis."[113] Like Hutchins, Whitehead, and Giamatti, Pelikan grounds his position on traditional Western intellectual tenets, such as the need for rediscovery of an authentic humanism grounded in a disciplined imagination, and "the instinctive faith that there is an Order of Nature which can be traced in every detailed occurrence."[114] Pelikan does not appear to confront squarely the degree of confusion and conflict over the idea that inquiry is progressive that currently exists in higher education. Nor does he explicitly come to terms with his own call for a fundamental reorganization of the university.[115] While some of the ideas that he advances to accommodate contemporary concerns are thoughtful, in general they seem to be predicated on the assumption that the university can meet challenges and overcome conflicts by simply absorbing new realms of thought.

It is possible that the much discussed incoherence of both the pursuit and the transmission of knowledge in higher education is partly a consequence of the insufficiency of these visions and others even for manifesting the actual state of knowledge. Perhaps the confusion is at least partly due to the idea that the aims grounded in the past, and the emphasis placed on unity based on past pronouncements do not adequately speak to the contemporary pursuit of knowledge. If that is the case, then simply reforming or revising them, as Pelikan attempts to do, is not adequate.

The fact that Pelikan does not address postmodern critiques of knowledge may be symptomatic of a larger oversight among defenders of higher education and in the multitude of contemporary critiques of higher education. In the next two chapters, I will analyze postmodern critiques of the idea that inquiry is progressive by five prominent postmodern philosophers: Jean-Francois Lyotard, Richard Rorty, Calvin Schrag, the late Michel Foucault, and Jacques Derrida. I will show how each philosopher argues that the relationship between aims pronounced in the past, present inquiry, and progress toward future realization is an unduly limiting basis for the pursuit of knowledge, before pursuing the consequences of my analyses in Chapters 5 and 6.

NOTES

1. Robert Maynard Hutchins, *The Conflict in Education in a Democratic Society* (Westport, Conn.: Greenwood Press, 1972, first published 1953), 71.
2. Robert Maynard Hutchins, *Education for Freedom* (New York: Grove, 1963, first published 1943), 85.
3. Robert Maynard Hutchins, *The Higher Learning in America* (New Haven: Yale University Press, 1936).
4. Ibid., 73.
5. Ibid., 63.
6. Ibid.
7. Ibid.
8. Ibid., 63, 78, 79, 81, 85.
9. Ibid., 59.
10. Ibid., 57.
11. Ibid., 92.
12. Ibid., 95.
13. Ibid., 97–98.
14. Ibid., 106–108. This organization also provides the structure for the third and fourth year of undergraduate study. This study is comprised of the fundamental problems of metaphysics (first principles, natural philosophy, philosophy of man), the social sciences (practical principles of ethics, politics, and economics), and the natural sciences. In *Higher Learning*, Hutchins also advocated that the departmental system and professional schools be abolished. Ibid., 111–112.
15. *Education for Freedom*, chap. 3.
16. Ibid., 85.
17. Ibid., 92.
18. Ibid., 100.
19. *The Conflict in Education*, 102–103.
20. Ibid., 106.
21. Robert Maynard Hutchins, *Great Books: The Foundation of a Liberal Education* (New York: Simon and Schuster, 1954), 4.
22. Ibid., 26–27.
23. Ibid., 29–30.
24. Ibid., 9.
25. Ibid.
26. Robert Maynard Hutchins, *The University of Utopia* (Chicago: University of Chicago Press, 1964, first published 1953).
27. Ibid., 56, 67–68.
28. Ibid., 70.
29. Robert Maynard Hutchins, *The Learning Society* (New York: Praeger, 1968), chap. 7.
30. Ibid., 135–136.
31. Alfred North Whitehead, "The Aims of Education," in *The Aims of Education and Other Essays* (New York: Macmillan, 1967, first published, 1929), 3.
32. Alfred North Whitehead, *Process and Reality: An Essay in Cosmology* (New York: Macmillan, 1929), 28–29; Alfred North Whitehead, *Adventures of Ideas* (New York: Collier Macmillan, 1967, first published 1933), 209; Alfred North Whitehead,

"The Rhythmic Claims of Freedom and Discipline," in *Aims of Education*, 34.

33. "The Aims of Education" and "The Rhythmic Claims of Freedom and Discipline," in *Aims of Education*, 3, 32.

34. "The Rhythmic Claims of Freedom and Discipline," in *Aims of Education*, 32.

35. Alfred North Whitehead, *The Function of Reason* (Princeton: Princeton University Press, 1929), 11.

36. Ibid.

37. Ibid., 37–38.

38. Ibid., 48.

39. Ibid., 28–29.

40. Ibid., 37.

41. Ibid., 11–12.

42. Ibid., 17–19, 40.

43. Ibid., 40–41.

44. Ibid., 65.

45. Ibid., 80.

46. Ibid., 42–43.

47. Ibid., 43.

48. Ibid., 43–44.

49. Ibid., 49, 50.

50. "The Aims of Education," in *Aims of Education*, 3.

51. Ibid., 4.

52. Ibid.

53. *Function of Reason*, 80.

54. Ibid., 7–8.

55. Ibid., 80–81.

56. "The Rhythmic Claims of Freedom and Discipline," in *Aims of Education*, 39.

57. "The Aims of Education," in *Aims of Education*, 1.

58. "The Rhythmic Claims of Freedom and Discipline," in *Aims of Education*, 39.

59. "The Aims of Education," in *Aims of Education*, 5.

60. Ibid., 6–7.

61. "The Place of Classics in Education," in *Aims of Education*, 72.

62. "The Rhythm of Education," in *Aims of Education*, 25–26.

63. "The Place of Classics in Education," in *Aims of Education*, 61.

64. Ibid., 74.

65. Ibid., 75.

66. "Technical Education and its Relation to Science and Literature," in *Aims of Education*, 47.

67. Ibid., 48.

68. "The Aims of Education," in *Aims of Education*, 10–13.

69. A. Bartlett Giamatti, *A Free and Ordered Space: The Real World of the University* (New York: W. W. Norton, 1988), 12.

70. "On Congregations, their Pleasures and Perils," in *A Free and Ordered Space*, 92.

71. A. Bartlett Giamatti, "The Nature and Purpose of the University," in *The University and the Public Interest* (New York: Atheneum, 1981), 17.

72. Ibid.

73. Ibid., 18.
74. Ibid., 18–19.
75. "On Behalf of the Humanities," in *University and the Public Interest*, 49–50.
76. "Sentimentality," in *University and the Public Interest*, 47–48.
77. "Nature Justly Viewed," in *University and the Public Interest*, 60–61.
78. Ibid., 68; "Sentimentality," in *University and the Public Interest*, 47.
79. "A City of Green Thoughts," in *Free and Ordered Space*, 135–136.
80. Ibid.
81. "The Earthly Use of a Liberal Education," in *Free and Ordered Space*, 123.
82. "A City of Green Thoughts," in *Free and Ordered Space*, 132.
83. Ibid., 132–133.
84. "On Behalf of the Humanities," in *University and the Public Interest*, 49–50.
85. "A City of Green Thoughts," in *Free and Ordered Space*, 130.
86. "On Behalf of the Humanities," in *University and the Public Interest*, 50.
87. "Give Time to Time," in *Free and Ordered Space*, 301–302.
88. "The Earthly Use of a Liberal Education," in *Free and Ordered Space*, 120; "The Apocalyptic Style," in *University and the Public Interest*, 38.
89. "The Private University and the Public Interest," in *Free and Ordered Space*, 216.
90. "A Family of Freedoms and Responsibilities," in *Free and Ordered Space*, 82–83; *University and the Public Interest*, viii–ix.
91. "On Behalf of the Humanities," in *University and the Public Interest*, 58.
92. Ibid., 56, 54.
93. "Nature Justly Viewed," in *University and the Public Interest*, 74, 75.
94. "A Liberal Education and the New Coercion," in *Free and Ordered Space*, 110.
95. Jaroslav Pelikan, *The Idea of the University: A Reexamination* (New Haven: Yale University Press, 1992), 87.
96. John Henry Newman, *The Idea of a University Defined and Illustrated*: I. In Nine Discourses Delivered to the Catholics of Dublin [1852]; II. In Occasional Lectures and Essays Addressed to the Members of the Catholic University [1858], edited with introduction and notes by I. T. Ker. (Oxford: Clarendon, 1976).
97. Pelikan, *Idea of the University*, 16–17, 32, 76, 117.
98. Ibid., 30.
99. Ibid., 48.
100. Ibid., 64, 122–123.
101. Ibid., 50.
102. Ibid., 153, 159–167, 161, 163.
103. Ibid., 152–53.
104. Ibid., chap. 13, 139, 144–145.
105. Ibid., 67.
106. Ibid., 145.
107. Ibid., 64.
108. Ibid., 65.
109. Ibid., 105.
110. Ibid., 108–109.
111. Ibid., 103, 195–197.

112. Ibid., 82.
113. Ibid., 9–10, chap. 2.
114. Ibid., 18, 50–51.
115. Ibid., 108.

3

Lyotard, Rorty, and Schrag:
The Search for New Grounds for Inquiry

In this chapter, I will begin to show the significance of postmodern critique for inquiry. Postmodern critique calls into question the efficacy of the assumption that the organized pursuit of knowledge is essentially an endeavor that progresses toward desirable aims that originate in the past. It stakes this position on the claim that basic deficiencies are apparent in the overall course of inquiry, and that an appropriate response to these deficiencies requires a rethinking of the nature and aims of inquiry. The claim is not that inquiry has been unsuccessful at producing knowledge, if "knowledge" is understood to signify what it conventionally means to scholars. Rather, the claim is that generally, the pursuit of knowledge as it is conventionally conceived and practiced has reached a point of stasis, at least when considered against the larger aims that I have presented.

If postmodern critique ended here, as its critics tend to conclude, then perhaps their allegations of nihilism would be justified. However, the critics of postmodern thought have not recognized the most important aspect of these critiques. This aspect emerges if the critiques are understood in the context of inquiry. Postmodern critique does not end with the claim that the modern pursuit of knowledge has reached intractable limitations. This claim is its starting point. The greatest importance of postmodern critique is that it uses the claim of modern limitations as an opportunity to encourage scholars to think differently about what it means to engage in an inquiry and to engage in the practice of inquiry differently. As I will show, these critiques can be interpreted to provide ideas that can serve as the basis for a viable and robust alternative to conventional ideas of inquiry, although none of the philosophers examined here have developed such an alternative. My aim in this chapter and the next is to elicit the most important elements of these critiques that can serve as the raw material that I will use in order to "think differently" about inquiry, and to develop an alternative concept of inquiry.

My analysis of the critiques of Lyotard, Rorty, Schrag, Foucault, and Derrida, respectively, will be presented as follows. First, I will describe the critique of progress in each case. I will focus on the alleged deficiencies that have emerged in the relationship between inquiry, progress, and the social good in the modern era, and that are alleged to have damaged the potential of this relationship to the extent that other ways of conceptualizing and structuring inquiry should be considered. I will then explore the various consequences of each critique for an alternative concept of inquiry.

LYOTARD: DYNAMIC INQUIRY

> What, then, is the postmodern? . . . It is undoubtedly a part of the modern. . . . Postmodernism thus understood is not modernism at its end but in the nascent state, and this state is constant.[1]

While the postmodern critique of inquiry and knowledge is not comprised of a single theoretical position, the work of French philosopher Jean-Francois Lyotard is critically regarded as a major voice in this contemporary critique. *The Postmodern Condition: A Report on Knowledge* is considered to be an important work because it articulates a perceived condition of inquiry and offers a historical and social account of its emergence. An understanding of Lyotard's critique of progress requires that one understand what Lyotard means by the terms "language games," "legitimation," "metanarrative," "postmodern science," and "performativity" as he develops these concepts in *Condition*.

Language Games and Science

All forms of knowledge embody patterns of linguistic expression between people: to know is to engage in discourse or acts of communication. For example, we use language to assert and describe what is true. When we make truth assertions and attempt to support them with evidence and argument, and if we are using language according to convention, our discourse follows linguistic rules specific to truth assertions.

Following Ludwig Wittgenstein, whose late work is the basis for this approach to understanding language as being, in effect, the ground of knowledge, Lyotard refers to the form of communication involved in truth assertions as a kind of "language game." All human communication can be understood as embodying different kinds of language games. The object of different language games is to win in the sense of realizing a desired outcome. Lyotard claims that while language games are not the exclusive basis for understanding social relations, they are the minimum relation required for a society to exist.[2]

The rules of the language game that concerns truth, as in all language games, are the basis of a contract, which may or may not be explicit, among the participants.[3] The "contract" is simply the rules of the kind of game that is being played. The process of scientific proof is one version of the language game of truth with its own rules, which vary among and within fields of inquiry. It is conventional that the designation of a truth proposition as knowledge requires that the idea be confirmed as such by being submitted to some form of verification as agreed upon by experts. Scientific knowledge requires that a true statement be experimentally verifiable according to the language of specialists in a given scientific field.[4]

Lyotard claims that although scientific or experimentally verifiable knowledge is only one kind of truth-game, since the Enlightenment its success in producing knowledge has given it widely acknowledged social status as the basis of truth per se, rather than being one kind of truth. However, this status has also generated a problem. The problem for scientists and other interested parties is how to continually legitimize, or retain authorization for, determining what shall count as science. Lyotard equates the social authorization of science to the social authorization of civil legislation: both are forms of legitimation. In the latter instance, legitimation is the authorization vested in public officials to issue laws that govern human behavior. In order for a statement to be law, it must be issued by certain people (elected or appointed officials) and it must be developed and put into effect according to certain rules of procedure. Similarly, in the case of scientific knowledge, legitimation refers to the authorization vested in scientists to determine what counts as scientific.[5]

The language game of scientific knowledge requires a rationale on which it can be legitimized, and thus accepted by society, as an authoritative basis of understanding reality, just as ideas of justice require a rationale for society's acceptance. Lyotard claims that in both cases resort is made to narrative, or a fictional story, as the basis of legitimation.[6] Narratives determine criteria of competence and illustrate how they must be applied. They define what can be done and said.[7] For example, Lyotard claims that Plato's "Allegory of the Cave" in *The Republic* serves the function of legitimizing dialectical inquiry as the classical truth-game, by telling a story about the virtue of knowledge.[8]

Critique of Metanarrative

Although Lyotard believes that different kinds of language games are incommensurable with each other, he claims that how the game of science is legitimized has particular historical, intellectual, and social significance. In the modern period science has been legitimized in the West by two overarching stories, or what Lyotard calls "metanarratives." In the "political" version, epitomized by the French Third Republic, science is legitimized as the means of emancipating the people from political domination.[9] In this story, scientific knowledge tells the universal metasubject, "the people," who are supposedly self-governing, what is possible.[10] Science serves a wholly practical function, supplying information for the practical ends of the collectivity. This version, although still active in public discourse, became delegitimized, according to Lyotard, when it was realized that science can only play its own game. Since science cannot play the game of prescriptive statements, it cannot be grounded in a metanarrative about the just State.[11] The second alternative, which Lyotard calls "philosophical," originated in the founding of the University of Berlin early in the nineteenth century and came to be philosophically expressed most prominently in German idealism.[12] In this mostly Hegelian version, as Lyotard depicts it, science is itself the metasubject and legitimizes itself through the historical unfolding of reason.[13] In the course of this story, the people and the State are indirectly legitimized, as embodiments of reason. According to Lyotard, the German version collapsed because its metaphysical foundation was revealed to be unscientific.[14]

In the wake of the decline of these two metanarratives, in the twentieth century, some philosophers of science, so-called logical positivists, attempted to legitimize science on the basis of the authority of the rules of scientific verification themselves. These philosophers gained prominence by attempting to determine a perfect metalanguage, formal logic.[15] However, it was eventually realized that, for any formal system to account for all phenomena and remain consistent, it must be grounded on assumptions that cannot themselves be demonstrated. Thus, no formal language can be universal and remain consistent.

Lyotard claims that in the aftermath of this failure to legitimize scientific method as the means of yielding certain, universal truths, at least some scientists and philosophers began to think very differently. They began to think that reality and knowledge involve paradoxes that scientific explanation had to account for, rather than overcome. Thus, the legitimation of scientific knowledge was drastically altered to account for the paradoxes that emerge because of the internal limitations of formal systems.[16] The concept of a metalanguage was replaced by the principle of a plurality of inconsistent languages, and thus a plurality of incommensurable truths.

Postmodern science—by concerning itself with such things as undecidables, the limits of precise control, conflicts characterized by incomplete information, *"fracta,"* catastrophes, and pragmatic paradoxes—is theorizing its own evolution as discontinuous, catastrophic, nonrectifiable, and paradoxical. It is changing the meaning of the word *knowledge,* while expressing how such a change can take place. It is producing not the known, but the unknown.[17]

It is important to make clear that Lyotard is placing significance on the appearance of these concepts in scientific inquiry, rather than resting his case on a judgment by himself that these subjects are "good" science. He believes that the appearance of these concepts in science signals a fundamental change, what the late Thomas Kuhn would call a scientific revolution or paradigm change.[18] It does not diminish this claim to acknowledge that some, if not all, of these concepts have not achieved widespread currency among scientists. Lyotard is witnessing the appearance of these concepts in science as an interested observer and claiming that (1) since they embody perspectives about reality and science that, at least until now, most scientists would consider to be very unscientific, and (2) since they are attracting a good number of believers in the scientific community, therefore, (3) they suggest that a fundamental change in inquiry is taking place.

For Lyotard, this "postmodern condition" of the preeminent language game means that the phenomena of the world that science investigates, the "external world," is essentially unpredictable and unstable. In this situation, all that can be calculated is the probability that a scientist's truth proposition will say one thing rather than another.[19] The goal of the game of postmodern science is to discover the rules governing the behavior of particular phenomena that break generally accepted rules, rather than to make discoveries that contribute toward an increasingly complete, accurate, and consistent picture of what nature really is as a unified whole. Under the new circumstances, we can know "islands of determinism" rather than a single, stable continent.[20] Inquiry seeks reasons to justify the creation of new games that are contingent on rules that apply in only highly particularized conditions.

Critique of Performativity

Lyotard claims that after the decline of metanarrative and logical positivism, another new version of the science game has become legitimized. He calls this game "performativity," or the principle of optimizing performance by technological innovation.[21] Given the limitations of the human senses and the increasing complexity of empirical demonstration and proof, the principle of replication has become increasingly dependent on sophisticated and expensive technology. The rules of technological application in capitalist society, argues Lyotard, enforce a game of efficiency. The production of scientific proof costs significant sums of money, with the result that scientists who can maximize output (proof) while minimizing input expended in the process of proof (energy, and thus cost) are most likely to receive research funds (although Lyotard acknowledges that there are exceptions). The pursuit of scientific knowledge becomes a force not for its own end but as an instrument for maximizing market power and economic wealth. In this game, optimal performance is the basis of legitimation.[22]

Lyotard alleges that this game has demoralized research scientists and has forced the university into a subordinate, functional role in the social system. The loss of metanarrative as basis of the legitimation of science is a "crisis of the university institution that in the past relied on it."[23] The principle of optimal performance affects not only the pursuit of knowledge but the nature of its transmission as well.[24] "The speculative hierarchy of learning gives way to an immanent and, as it were, flat network of areas of inquiry, the respective frontiers of which are in constant flux . . . and the universities lose their function of speculative legitimation."[25]

Thus, according to Lyotard, higher education has become increasingly defined by its capacity to create and produce skills indispensable to competition in world markets and the efficient maintenance of internal social cohesion, whereas according to the modern metanarratives, the education of elites was for the purpose of creating leaders for the emancipation or realization of society.[26] The goal of learning becomes problem-solving in the "here-and-now" and skill at organizing data "into an efficient strategy."[27] For Lyotard, this situation entails the demise of "the Professor," because "a professor is no more competent than memory bank networks in transmitting established knowledge, no more competent than interdisciplinary teams in imagining new moves or new games."[28]

Lyotard thinks that the decline of metanarrative is a good thing, because he believes that these epics of progress have turned out to be frauds: they have resulted in totalitarianism and mass exploitation. "The nineteenth and twentieth centuries have given us as much terror as we can take. We have paid enough price for the nostalgia of the whole and the one."[29] Further, he sees some positive aspects to performativity as legitimation, but claims that ultimately its results are destructive, because performativity follows a systems theory logic: whatever course of action increases the overall efficiency of the social system is legitimated, without decisive regard for its effects on human beings.[30] Moreover, Lyotard claims that this kind of systems theory does not work, because it is predicated on the notion that a system can be stabilized and can yield perfect information and is thus subject to prediction and control, which is contradicted by the rules of the postmodern game of science, summarized above, that there is only local determinism.[31]

Critique of Modern Aims

The critique of metanarrative suggests that there are problems with the association of modern inquiry and the aims that I presented in the preceding chapter. The pursuit of truth and science represent two versions of Lyotard's philosophical metanarrative. The belief that inquiry progresses toward realization of knowledge of the whole and the notion that ideas are legitimized by scientific verification, thereby contributing to a historical "progress of ideas" that advances civilization, implies that reality is stable or evolves systematically in time, instead of it exhibiting what is, for Lyotard, an ultimately inexplicable multiplicity. For Lyotard, to make moves is "to set the imagination to work," but the work of imagination is not to further the progress of ideas.[32] Further, reason as a function of modern system theory reflects an outmoded modern dichotomy between functional reason and critical reason, a dichotomy that, like progress, Lyotard associates with the metanarrative-based legitimation of knowledge.[33] Instead, postmodern reason is defined by "the principle of a plurality" of scientific languages.[34]

The notions of progress associated with democracy and humanity would be, for Lyotard, versions of the political metanarrative. The idea that one learns how to be a free citizen, capable of contributing to the realization of democracy, by learning the meaning of free inquiry as it is expressed in the languages of the liberal arts, mythologizes knowledge as an emancipation of "the people." Similarly, the attempt to accommodate the notion of "knowledge its own end" to progressive social change while retaining modern ideas of the nature of knowledge and the modern research university also subscribes to the outdated political metanarrative.

Moreover, in the myth of the authentic, whole human being that is implied in their works, all of the modern thinkers make the mistake of conflating language games. While there is a "strict interlinkage between the kind of language called science and the kind called ethics and politics," the linkage is social, not linguistic.[35] Since these games are comprised of different kinds of statements, denotative and prescriptive, respectively, their rules are different: justice cannot be derived from the scientific, nor can the scientific be derived from the just.[36] Justice cannot be resolved in terms of theoretical models: current practice establishes context, and the question of justice can only be addressed on a case-by-case basis.[37] As is the case with scientific knowledge, then, ethical knowledge is local knowledge.[38]

Inquiry as Dynamic Intellectual Activity

If the idea of inquiry grounded in progress toward aims established in the past is subject to the failure of metanarrative, what alternative idea of inquiry might emerge from Lyotard's critique? A starting point for this alternative is suggested by Lyotard's definition of knowledge. He calls this idea of knowledge "pragmatic." Knowledge in the pragmatic sense is competency in playing language games, and this competency applies to not only the scientific language game, but many others.[39]

This idea of knowledge implies an emphasis on inquiry as an intellectual activity rather than on the production of outcomes that advance or improve upon a received body of knowledge. This perspective follows from Lyotard's focus on the direction that scientific theory is moving, namely, a growing recognition that aspects of reality behave paradoxically rather than consistently, and that there are good reasons why this behavior is not merely a surface appearance that is ultimately explainable in terms of orderly laws. On this basis, the end of inquiry would be to create or discover new rules that depart from established ones, thereby providing bases for inquiry to move in new, unpredictable directions, rather than to contribute to a growing body of consistent rules.

This idea of dynamic inquiry is also supported by Lyotard's assertion that postmodernism is modernism in its "nascent" state.[40] Lyotard focuses especially, though not exclusively, on distinguishing postmodern from modern aesthetics, but his idea of nascence is intended to apply to postmodern thought in general. However, he does not develop an extended meaning for this idea that is particularly illuminating. Nascence generally refers to something's being born or coming into being, thus to its initial state. In chemistry, for example, nascence designates the state of an element immediately after it has been released from a compound and having unusual chemical activity because atoms of the element have not yet combined to form molecules.

I interpret Lyotard's notion of nascence, along with his statement that the postmodern is that which in the modern is unpresentable, as meaning that inquiry informed by postmodern critique places emphasis on allowing intellect very broad prerogative to determine the directions that inquiry may go, rather than on maintaining a line of inquiry that is consistent with ends or objectives that are determined in advance of the activity. From the standpoint of the individual who seeks knowledge, the emphasis is on the idea that one is an inquirer before one is a knower. Knowledge is not something one accumulates but is instead something one uses to create new ideas. Lyotard's idea of knowledge as "pragmatic," diverse competencies also supports this idea of inquiry, since it emphasizes intellectual agility, or skills at adapting to new contexts. It also suggests that a good inquirer cultivates the ability to recognize when opportunities for new paths become possible and to alter the course of inquiry in ways that create such opportunities.

This kind of inquiry would be experimental rather than innovative; the latter is "but a way of repeating, without great difference, something that already has been done and that has worked."[41] For Lyotard, an experiment is an imaginative revision of received knowledge, a new move in a language game in which one is always an addressee before one is a sender. Further, the inquirer seeks to come "to grips with the new effects produced by the new situation of a joint discussion."[42] The inquirer participates in dialogue with the understanding that the obligation to be a good listener precedes the freedom to experiment.[43] Inquiry is, then, both an experimental and a participatory act.

The inquirer does not seek to master a body of knowledge because language cannot be mastered: "its very plurality makes it impossible for anyone to establish her- or himself in a field and proceed to produce its laws in a sort of universal language."[44] Moreover, the idea of mastering a body of knowledge suggests that knowledge is stable and bounded. Perhaps most importantly, since the inquirer is essentially focused on departing from, rather than building upon, received ideas and theories, Lyotard's ideal is much more that of a critical questioner and debater than it is the ideal envisioned by the modernists that I have examined.[45]

Further, the structure of inquiry would be not be based on the notion that there is an order of knowledge that is permanent, or the notion that established knowledge carries the authority that is associated with the status given truth. Since for Lyotard the limits imposed by institutions on language games are never permanent, it seems that Lyotard would also reject the modern notion that knowledge expands within otherwise stable disciplines.[46] Instead, the structure would encourage "working at the limits of what the rules permit, in order to invent new moves, perhaps new rules and therefore new games."[47] It would also aim to minimize the possibility of one kind of inquiry prevailing over the other kinds, which leads to the domination of some groups of thinkers by others. The structure of both research and the curriculum would be to "maximize the multiplicity of small narratives."[48]

Since language games are of "striking disparity," it is not surprising to find that Lyotard rejects the interdisciplinary organization of knowledge, because it implies "common measures."[49] Interdisciplinary approaches are consistent with performativity because they emphasize users as beneficiaries of a "complex conceptual and material machinery."[50] Since different kinds of language games are not translatable, interdisciplinary knowledge can only be legitimated by performativity, which for Lyotard is the bane of higher learning. In contrast, the idea of language games "refines our sensitivity to differences and reinforces our capacity to tolerate the incommensurable."[51]

Individual, Community, and the Social Good

Lyotard's critique of technology and the negative influence that it has on basic experimental research is a theme that is often associated with traditional conceptions of "knowledge for its own end." Most importantly, I believe that Lyotard is seeking to create a new idea of what it means to be an individual intellectual against the rationalization of modern technocracy, and this concern is not new. What is relatively new with his postmodernist position is the notion that the intellectual is not "self-determined" but what I will call self-initiating—one seeks to create new grounds that can be used as points of departure, rather than to ground oneself in an original, authentic, and autonomous subject of inquiry. Lyotard rejects the notion of a "universal subject" because it assumes that one could step outside of language games and think at a metalinguistic level, thereby attaining an "exclusive and exhaustive" point of view, which is not possible.[52] Rather, the inquirer is pragmatic in the sense of being capable, and willing, to leave what was previously believed when new possibilities require it. It is an idea of the individual who does not merely resist being determined by a system through explaining its machinations, but responds to the system as raw material to be used to create languages that are no longer of the system.

What is nascent in the modern exponents of inquiry that connects with Lyotard is a concern that the intellectual be free to inquire wherever intellect may take it. Unlike the others, Lyotard's critique claims, and elaborates an argument to show why, the scholar is being overdetermined by the socioeconomic system. Lyotard advances a position that does not wax nostalgic for metaphysical, that is, metanarrative foundations which, he claims, cannot realize the free mind but can only encumber it. In keeping language games local and forever subject to change and closure, by some act of any immediate participant, he seeks to reconstitute the realm of intellectual creativity so that the intellectual can make particular worlds, rather than limit itself by the illusory idea of making *the* world.

The idea of a single, unified community of free thinkers and the idea of a unified community of free citizens, so important to the visions of inquiry and progress for the modern thinkers, are, for Lyotard, fictions that can only result in the oppression of individuals. This notion is bound to be very difficult for many inquirers to accept. It is important to point out that a rejection of the idea of unity does not mean embracement of some kind of exclusionary ethos. The overall aim becomes diversification of inquiry.

This vantage point suggests that the loss of community in the university is partly explained by the fact that, amid the plethora of knowledge claims, the disciplinary matrix cannot directly influence the formation of a university community. The accumulation and expansion of knowledge perhaps defies the idea of community. In any case, a conception of inquiry informed by Lyotard's critique would likely reject the idea of a single university community that the individual inquirer is a part of, because it would retard the maximization of inquiries.[53]

If the idea of a unified intellectual community is not desirable, what are the implications for the idea that inquiry is consistent with, and advance, the social good? For Lyotard, the social good resides in the recognition that human society, like nature, is composed of "heteromorphous" language games rather than being a whole.[54] Any attempt toward achieving consensus by a new grand metanarrative to rescue humanity from system is out of the question, because such a project would invariably result in another oppressive system.[55] Postmodern science suggests that social assent can only be legitimately comprised of "little narratives," language games whose rules and play are "locally determined."[56] The social end of inquiry is not consensus, but an open society that allows for a multiplicity of divergent games and encourages the ongoing imaginative creation of new ones, that is, local relations among small numbers of players.[57]

The Search for New Directions

Clearly, a conception of inquiry informed by Lyotard's critique would enhance the potential for new paths that depart from established ones. It would make it possible for individual inquiries to move in unanticipated and unusual directions. The shift from the level of general aims to the local level of actual practice provides a fresh starting point for thinking about inquiry. This starting point would emphasize inquiry as a dynamic, experimental intellectual activity that uses received knowledge for the purpose of creating new courses of inquiry. The dynamic and experimental sense of inquiry implied by Lyotard emphasizes inquiry as an intellectual activity that aims to undergo and produce change. Specifically, an inquiry that is successful would be one that shifts directions toward unpredictable, unprecedented forms of thought and practice, rather than being an activity that is successful if it produces results that essentially build upon or replace the results of previous inquiries.

However, a well-developed conception must provide for inquiry to do something more than depart from what is known. This conception must provide some general direction for inquiry, without imposing the limitations of metanarrative. Even if emphasis is placed on activity over outcomes, it must provide an idea of what is produced or obtained as a consequence of creating new courses of inquiry. It must also give reasons why the creation of new courses of inquiry is worthwhile. Lyotard's critique does not provide guidance concerning what is obtained in these departures and its worth.

Further, it must have some societal worth to be justified, if for no other reason than the fact that higher education is financed largely through public funds. Even if Lyotard rejects the idea of the whole, he does advance an idea of the social good. Yet the idea of local inquiry needs to have some basis for enhancing the capacity or potential of inquiry to contribute more directly to the social good beyond the immediate benefits to the actual participants of an inquiry.

RORTY: PRACTICAL INQUIRY

> I argue that the attempt (which has defined traditional philosophy) to explicate "rationality" and "objectivity" in terms of conditions of accurate representation is a self-deceptive effort to eternalize the normal discourse of the day, and that, since the Greeks, philosophy's self-image has been dominated by this attempt.[58]

While American philosopher Richard Rorty agrees with Lyotard's assertion that a new metanarrative is not what the West needs, he makes a sharp distinction between what he believes it needs and what he thinks Lyotard represents.[59] Rorty claims to reject metanarratives for the down-to-earth reason that they are "an unhelpful distraction from what Dewey calls 'the meaning of the daily detail.'"[60]

Critique of Epistemology

To understand Rorty's position on knowledge and what it means for inquiry, one must understand the basis for his break from the analytic philosophical tradition and his postmodern interpretation of Deweyan pragmatism, which was established with *Philosophy and the Mirror of Nature*. In that book, Rorty claims that Western philosophy, especially Anglo-American philosophy, has pursued a mistaken notion of truth, the idea that truth refers to something objective and eternal. For Rorty, truth is better thought of as a name or label for the subject of agreement among any group of humans concerning beliefs, values, and action. Rorty locates the origin of the allegedly mistaken view with the Platonic distinction between Forms, embodying permanent, unchanging, universal Ideas and accessible only by the intellect, and the transient flux of particular things experienced by the senses.[61]

Rorty argues that this distinction began as an arbitrary story by Plato about general truths that are intelligible by the divine intellect based on a visual metaphor of the human eye; then, Aristotle developed this story in more detail by describing a process through which this Eye of the Mind internalized such forms in harmony with the Reason of Nature.[62] Descartes substantially revised this narrative by saying that the intellect represents the world, so that the clear and distinct reason of the immaterial human mind, not the Reason of Nature, became the foundation of truth.[63] Then Locke developed the Cartesian story further, by emphasizing and elaborating sense representations as primary ideas, and Kant revised the story again, by moving the ground of knowledge from outer objects to inner, transcendent structures of the mind.[64]

Like many philosophers since Kant, Rorty claims to expose flaws in the arguments that each philosopher makes. Whereas most philosophers would, by virtue of these flaws, locate problems to solve, or ideas to replace with a superior conception of knowledge as a relation between human knower and object, Rorty claims that these flaws merely indicate that the arguments are essentially manners of speaking, employing different vocabularies.[65]

He takes particular aim at the modern notion that to know is to represent accurately, and he disputes representationalist problems, from which has emerged epistemology, the very core of contemporary analytic philosophy and the foundation of the sciences.[66] Rorty argues that the problems of justification arising from the story of knowledge as representation have not been overcome by subsequent anti-Cartesian philosophers. Philosophers are "still committed to the construction of a permanent, neutral framework for inquiry, and thus for all of culture" that "can be isolated prior to the conclusion of inquiry."[67] They will not, in Rorty's opinion, be able to isolate certain representations, expressions, or processes as basic, "except on the basis of a prior knowledge within which these elements occur."[68] Thus, he asserts that it is time for philosophers to abandon this misguided epistemological project.

Instead, asserts Rorty, they should follow the lead of Dewey and the later Wittgenstein and release their creative intellects from the self-imposed limitations caused by the optional notion that knowledge needs foundations, or a theory.[69] Philosophical thought should be "edifying" rather than systematic:

"the ways things are said is more important than the possession of truths."[70] Rational certainty is most *usefully* understood as a matter of victory in argument, rather than an epistemological encounter that uncovers nonhuman reality.[71] For Rorty, knowing a proposition is true is not identified with being caused to do something by an object; rather, truth assertions can be justified only by social context.[72] Quoting philosopher Donald Davidson, Rorty argues that the meaning of words does not transcend "their systematic effect on the meanings of sentences in which they occur."[73] Thus, philosophers should see "*conversation* as the ultimate context within which knowledge is to be understood."[74]

Edification and Abnormal Discourse

The kind of conversation Rorty desires is "hermeneutic," which, for Rorty, means that "relations between various discourses [are] strands in a possible conversation" that assumes no disciplinary matrix that unites the participants.[75] In this kind of conversation, the elements will be based on an understanding of practice.[76]

Borrowing from the late Thomas Kuhn's account of scientific revolutions, Rorty introduces a distinction between "normal" and "abnormal" discourse. For normal discourse, there is consensus among participants concerning the rules that must be followed in order for a question, answer, or argument to be considered. In contrast, an abnormal discourse breaks the rules. "The product of abnormal discourse can be anything from nonsense to intellectual revolution, and there is no discipline which describes it, any more than there is a discipline devoted to the unpredictable, or of "creativity."[77]

The distinction between normal and abnormal discourse is not a distinction between subject matter or between methods. Any topic can be discoursed about abnormally.[78] From this perspective, Rorty dissolves the distinctions between fact and value, making and finding, objective and subjective, and, perhaps most controversial, the distinction between science and nonscience as well.[79] Further, the distinction between the values of science and the values of other realms of thought is not based on the idea that science uses uniquely objective and rational standards, nor on the basis of its subject matter. Rather, its value distinctions are a result of cultural considerations, "a function of educational and institutional patterns."[80]

Remaking

Rorty asserts that hermeneutics, as he has defined it, is not another way of knowing, but "another way of coping."[81] To elaborate this idea, Rorty borrows the theme of *Bildung*, which he translates as "self-formation," from Hans-Georg Gadamer. For Rorty, this means that education, properly conceived, is about "remaking" oneself rather than about "getting the facts right."[82] Education as edification is hermeneutic: one seeks to use ideas, via reading, research, talking, and writing, to create abnormal discourse in order to remake oneself.[83] The inquirer, then, copes with living by using its intellect to keep the conversation going, by changing the conversation. "For edifying discourse is *supposed* to be abnormal, to take us out of our old selves by the power of strangeness, to aid us in becoming new beings."[84]

Rorty interprets Gadamer's notion that education should have no goals outside itself to mean that differences between vocabularies are a function of their connections to different periods, traditions, and historical accidents.[85] Edification does not mean finding normal discourses to make oneself.[86] Thus, for Rorty inquiry does not mean, as it does for Giamatti, learning the various discourses of the humanities tradition for their own sake. Instead, one would learn them as the raw material for remaking oneself via the creation of new (abnormal) discourses.[87] Inquiry for Rorty is practical in the sense that a good inquirer is able to participate in conversation and edification, the creation of abnormal discourse and its introduction into participatory conversation.[88]

Contra Hutchins and Giamatti, the study of Great Books should be, at the college level, "remedial work."[89] For Rorty a Great Conversation is not normal discourse; instead, it is the activity of participating in what might be called a postmodern dialectic, in which abnormal discourse is created and heard from the point of view of normal discourse, with the goal of the abnormal becoming normal. Rorty claims that it is creative intellect, Whitehead's speculative Reason, that is the stuff of civilization. Unlike Whitehead, however, Rorty does not require scientific method to make speculative thought useful. Moreover, he would entirely reject Hutchins's and Whitehead's metaphysical presuppositions. Instead, "free and leisured conversation generates abnormal discourse as the sparks fly upward."[90]

Languages as Tools

Rorty states that edification is pragmatic. The point of edification, at least as it pertains to philosophers, is "to perform the social function which Dewey called breaking the crust of convention." For Rorty this means that edification should "prevent people from deluding themselves with the notion that people can know themselves, or anything else, except under "optional descriptions.""[91] Rorty values Dewey as a social philosopher because he "turns away from the theoretical scientists to the engineers and the social workers—the people who are trying to make people more comfortable and secure, and to use science and philosophy as tools for that purpose."[92]

On the question of the relationship between Rorty's notion of edification and his pragmatism, inferences can be made from his collection of essays, *Essays on Heidegger and Others*.[93] There he defines intellectual progress as "an increasing ability to shape the tools needed to help the species survive, multiply, and transform itself."[94] For Rorty, language is "a set of tools rather than a set of representations—tools which . . . change their users and the products of their use."[95] This approach is present when the inquirer "begins to take the relativity of thinghood to choice of description for granted, and so starts asking how to be useful rather than how to be right."[96]

Rorty appears to believe that as soon as the inquirer drops truth-as-representation this person will then seek to make its intellect practical to humanity. This conclusion is not at all apparent. If meaning is endlessly alterable through the recontextualization of signs, this does not mean that the meaning of words in abnormal discourse will gravitate toward practice and utility, unless the free thinker, or the community of free thinkers, limits the possibility of abnormal discourse to ideas that have practical import which alters the practical significance of academic freedom profoundly.[97]

Rorty's desire to defer abnormal discourse to its practical effects is further evidenced by the "pragmatic" use of language:

The pragmatist . . . thinks of the thinker as serving the community, and of his thinking as futile unless it is followed up by a reweaving of the community's web of belief. That reweaving will assimilate, by gradually literalizing, the new metaphors which the thinker has provided.[98]

The inquirer uses metaphors to change the languages that society speaks, thus enabling it to remake itself in some progressive manner. "Literalizing" metaphors means having them adopted as useful tools for social progress. In other words, it means normalizing abnormal discourse. For Rorty, social progress means making "things easier for everybody."[99]

It seems that what separates abnormal discourse as intellectual revolution from abnormal discourse as nonsense is the former's utility in helping society to overcome linguistic patterns of habitual use or modes of thinking, speaking, and acting that make life more wearisome and dull, and to replace them with patterns that allow people to remake themselves. In this sense, a good inquirer would be a postmodernized Deweyan social engineer, a useful poet: the inquirer uses language creatively as the intellectual tool to help democracy remake itself, thereby effecting practical social change.

Inquiry and the Social Good

It is not apparent, however, that remaking necessarily makes things easier or more comfortable and secure. Many inquirers would claim the opposite. If one tries to reconcile Rorty's ideas, it seems that remaking expresses a creative power to overcome personal and social stagnation, the capacity to exert control over given circumstances, the ability to give shape to one's environment and meaning to one's life. If so, then Rorty's notion of practical wisdom has much in common with Dewey's progressive educational philosophy, such as the idea that the only valuable educative experience is one that consists of and in growth and the recognition that individual growth cannot be removed from its social context.[100]

Rorty recognizes that much of what is assumed normal to the Western heritage of ideas was initially abnormal to, and resisted by, that tradition. Rorty recognizes that if the Great Conversation, and the multiplicity of languages in the liberal arts, are democratic and free, then they are critical of what is given in that tradition, rather than merely serving to reproduce it by extension. For Rorty, if there is no abnormal discourse, there is no conversation. "Knowledge its own end" does not mean adherence to received knowledge and values. Rather, the inquirer must learn to create new ideas, that is, new languages or ways of thinking, about human experience; one must learn to be "parasitic" upon the given.[101] Unlike Hutchins, Giamatti, and "the political right," for Rorty the free mind is not predicated on the notion that freedom follows from truth; nor does truth follow from freedom, as it does for Whitehead, Pelikan, and "the political left."[102] According to Rorty, there is no true nature or true human nature for the free mind to aim for.[103] The free mind is a mind that creates and uses ideas to remake oneself, rather than one that seeks to find and know explanations.

Rorty's notions of hermeneutics, edification, and abnormal discourse and his critique of epistemology suggest that an alternative idea of inquiry would structure inquiry to encourage the genesis of abnormal inquiries, rather than being based on disciplines and/or interdisciplinary work. Under Rorty, the only reason to connect ideas, or subject matter, would be to keep the conversation going by creating "abnormal" inquiries and then normalizing them, rather than to unify learning.

This idea of inquiry takes Lyotard's idea of language games one step further in several ways. First, it recognizes that an alternative inquiry must not only depart from what is "normal"; it must also be shared, critiqued, and accepted by peers (normalized). The basis for intellectual community would seem to be located in this communicative movement from abnormal to normal, rather than in the outcome of an inquiry. It is important to point out that "normalization" does not necessarily mean that, in the process of gaining acceptance, the idea has itself been fundamentally changed to bring it into line with established ideas (although it could very well be changed considerably through critique). Rather, normalization means that the idea has gained the support of peers. On the other hand, the movement from abnormal to normal should not be thought of in terms of an a priori formula or a litmus test. It is a continuum that is a function of local practice, instead of a general distinction.

The second way that an idea of inquiry informed by Rorty's work enhances one based on Lyotard's is that it provides an aim for local inquiry beyond simply departing from received ideas of knowledge. This aim is the remaking of the inquirer(s). This notion suggests that the focus on local inquiry is a focus on intellectual activity as a meaningful personal life-experience. Presumably, only an exceptional inquiry could remake an inquirer in a profound sense. However, one could say that in any inquiry, the inquirer aims to have an intellectual experience of some kind that produces a change in the inquirer that is not simply the acquisition of new knowledge. More significantly, it is an intellectual experience that enhances the inquirer's perspective of reality in some way.

The focus on inquiry as an experience of the inquirer also recognizes that the first reason why an inquirer is attracted to engage in inquiry is that the inquirer values the pursuit of knowledge for what it does for the inquirer's quality of life. The idea of remaking also supports the idea that the individual inquirer is self-initiating rather than self-determined, if the former is understood as the initiation of an inquiry, whereas the latter implies a finished product. Rorty's position that it is more useful to think of disciplines as constituting different vocabularies that embody values, not facts, suggests that the kind of experience that one aims to have is one that introduces a new source of value to human experience, rather than one that adds facts to an established body of knowledge.

Third, an alternative informed by Rorty recognizes the need for inquiry to have some significant contribution to the social good greater than the immediate, local effects that may be provided by any single inquiry. Rorty recognizes that inquiry needs to do much more than it is currently doing for the social good. To his credit, he does not succumb to the impulse to reject all direct associations of local inquiry with the general social good on the basis that generalization can be oppressive because it overlooks individual and group differences. Rorty's position that it is more useful to think of disciplines as constituting different vocabularies that embody values, not facts, suggests that the kind of experience that one aims to have is one that adds value to human experience, rather than one that adds facts to an established body of knowledge. This position makes it possible for the outcomes of alternative inquiry to be useful beyond their personal value to the inquirer.

However, Rorty leaves the problem of how to reconcile the pursuit of abnormal inquiry and the remaking of the inquirer with advancement of the social good. If he means that the only inquiry that is valuable is utilitarian, then he would seem to neglect the value of 2600 years of inquiry "for its own sake." The persistence of this history suggests that a viable alternative for inquiry would enhance the possibility for social utility, not demand it. Further, the idea of abnormal inquiry is not sufficiently developed beyond the notion that it is unfamiliar and deviates from generally accepted ideas. Abnormal inquiry needs to be accompanied by an idea of rationality that supports and distinguishes it, rather than defines it essentially in terms of deviation from standard beliefs. This idea of rationality should make a more explicit connection between the value of an inquiry for the inquirer, on the one hand, and the value of the inquiry for the community, on the other.

SCHRAG: INTERPRETIVE INQUIRY

> How does it stand with rationality as we attempt to make our way about in a postmodern world?[104]

American philosopher Calvin Schrag, borrowing ideas from many contemporary thinkers of the Continental persuasion, articulates a "refigured" idea of reason that incorporates the basic claims of postmodern critique.[105] His position emphasizes Rorty's argument against the modern epistemological framework, that is, rejection of the assumption that knowledge production needs ahistorical foundations.[106] In common with Lyotard, upon whom he especially relies for his understanding of postmodern critique, Schrag rejects the legitimacy of metanarrative as the basis for the social legitimation of knowledge.[107] Like both Lyotard and Rorty, he claims that knowledge emerges and changes within an unstable multiplicity of social practices.

Critique of Progress: Transversal Reason

Schrag's critique of progress is focused on the concept of reason. He describes the conventional modern idea of reason as "vertical," in that the inquirer assumes that the source of true knowledge is "above" the flux of experience. The vertical metaphor would apply to the aims of truth, science, democracy, and humanity described in Chapter 2, since each of these aims is grounded on the position that there is an aim for inquiry that stands above and outside the activity of inquiry. In contrast to the vertical metaphor, Schrag depicts postmodern reason as "horizontal," or lacking the capacity to make truth determinations in the absence of absolute, ahistorical criteria.[108] Although he credits postmodern critique for recognizing the horizontal discontinuities in discourse and social practices, Schrag also rejects horizontal reason on the basis that it leaves intellect in a state of indeterminacy.

Given that knowledge arises in social experience, Schrag asserts "that rationality is 'transversal' to the multiplicity of our discursive and non-discursive practices."[109] By "transversal," Schrag means that reason can be understood as "lying across varying forms of discourse, modes of thought, and institutional practices."[110] Reason is thus "diagonal" to the various manifestations of personal and social forms of life.[111] The metaphor of the diagonal is used by Schrag in contrast to the modern vertical and the postmodern horizontal metaphors of reason.

Schrag states that transversal rationality lies between modernity and postmodernity and between universalism and particularism.[112] By this statement, Schrag means that it "effects a passage between the orthodoxy of sedimented belief-systems and institutional forms" and "normatized rules and procedures" on the one hand, and the "heterodoxy of changing beliefs and practices" and "revolutionary thought and action" on the other.[113] This idea shifts the locus of knowledge from Cartesian and Kantian consciousness to "patterns of discourse and action."[114] Thus, the vertical approach is itself revealed as a contingent strategy.[115] The subject and consciousness emerge from within social practices rather than originating outside them.[116]

To overcome postmodern indeterminacy, Schrag utilizes what he calls "communicative praxis."[117] Communicative praxis is "the holistic space in which our ongoing thought and action, language and speech, interplay."[118] It is the ever-changing ground from which Schrag claims philosophy and knowledge actually originate. Within this social space, the subject is "de-centered" or displaced from its modernist isolation as epistemology's foundation and is resituated intersubjectively as speaker, author, and actor.[119] Social practices are not explained by theory from above but are "performances of meaning." Similarly, theory is "contextualized concept formation" and is embedded within, rather than coming from outside, discourse and action.[120]

Schrag describes the process of knowledge-formation as having three aspects or "moments" within the social space of communicative praxis. These aspects provide structure to reason in the absence of a transcendent foundation.[121] They are discernment, articulation, and disclosure. Schrag's articulation of these episodes is very ambiguous. They can be summarized as follows. First, by "discernment," Schrag means that the knower, as a willing participant in a community, aligns its understanding with operative assumptions of the community, but dissents from those assumptions that result in a "tyranny of custom."[122] Criteria for knowledge emerge from the "play of perspectives and practices" and provide the basis for discernment, not certainty.[123] Second, by "articulation," Schrag means that meaning emerges via a "radical hermeneutic" of social interpretation in speaking and writing, and it is directed to listeners and readers who respond to and revise what is communicated.[124] Third, by "disclosure," Schrag means that the knower's interpretation is a consequence of its referring, or responding, to "that which is other" as it is revealed in everyday experience.[125]

For Schrag, the task of postmodern rationality, then, is to comprehend and articulate how social and communicative practices coalesce within experience.[126] The key point is that unity and integration of thought and of action are not inevitably lost in, but emerge from, the ever-changing flux of particularity and diversity in social experience. However, unity and integration are always contextual.[127] Nor does transversal reason ever achieve a coincidence with any social practice.[128] Local meanings are made within a background of discourses and actions that influence but do not absolutely determine them.[129] Thus there is "convergence without coincidence" in the interplay between the vertical and the horizontal.[130]

For Schrag, like Rorty, coming to know is not "getting it right." Rather, it is "a process of delimiting the authority of any particular interpretation and discerning the possibilities for the creation of new standpoints through dissent and a revision of perspectives."[131] Since reason is situated within historical and communal existence, all knowledge occurs within the context of community.[132] This position means that, contra modernity, knowledge is not separate from its communication.[133] Rhetoric is refigured by Schrag as being rational, in that the event of knowledge is the rhetorical act of giving good reasons to persuade through critique, articulation, and disclosure.[134]

Inquiry with the Other

Schrag states that the decisive feature of transversal reason is the intrusion and acknowledgment of difference.[135] He claims that by his scheme of transversal rationality, "The integrity of otherness—other forms of thought and other social practices—is maintained, accomplishing at once a better understanding of that which is one's own and a recognition of the need to make accommodations and adjustments in the response to the presence of that which is other."[136]

For Schrag, then, the inquirer is open to alien forms of thought and practice by virtue of and within communicative praxis. Inquirers seek to know by interpreting particular social practices against the current background assumptions of the community. Knowledge is never outside the community; it emerges through the knower's interactive participation in a community of knowers and in the larger community. Knowing is an act of communication, in which the knower is de-centered within communal dialogue. To know is to understand the other's social experience, even though "we never achieve an untrammeled, perfect, or ideal manner of speaking or mode of communication."[137]

The act of remaking the self is, then, also an act of remaking the community by interpreting, revising, and re-introducing transformed ideas. Knowledge does not evolve in a linear fashion, but one becomes a better participant by broadening one's experience of diverse ideas and by refining one's abilities to comprehend the specifics of divergent particulars: "Every context-dependency is situated within a wider context-interdependency."[138]

As for Lyotard and Rorty, for Schrag the inquirer is skilled at creating and using different languages and vocabularies. Schrag claims that transversal reason is operative across disciplines, genres of discourse, and culture spheres.[139] He does claim that with transversality much of the inquiry that occurs is within the arts and sciences.[140] He specifically identifies the diagonal metaphor in mathematics, physiology, anatomy, physics, philosophy, psychiatry, and literary studies.[141]

Apart from developing the concept philosophically, Schrag refrains from searching for a paradigm that would equate the concept across disciplines, stating that the particularities of its meaning in different disciplines should not be minimized.[142] However, in a way similar to that of Rorty, he does claim that, from the standpoint of radical hermeneutics, there is no striking distinction between the physical and social sciences, since the practices of both emerge from the context of a community of investigators.[143]

Following Lyotard and Rorty, Schrag argues against the legitimacy of a grand narrative or the need for a foundationalist concept of rationality to ground knowledge and justify the university. Assuming that rationality is plural across realms of thought, he advances two notions of reason that would nevertheless be operative across knowledge domains. They include reason as "a catalyst for critique and as a performance of evaluation."[144] First, reason must engage in critical analysis of "different modes of discourse and different forms of life."[145] Second, reason must make value judgments based on concrete, particular situations, rather than at "an abstract metalevel of inquiry."[146] Schrag identifies both of these notions with inherent goals of liberal learning, namely, the development of a critical mind and the development of ethical judgment.[147]

Schrag also describes what he calls a "new humanism."[148] It is based on the idea that "moral action, as it arises out of the dialectic of conflict and consensus within the space of *ethos*, exhibits an operating intentionality of moral insight and self-understanding that antedates the construction both of value properties and of a monadic ethical subject that entertains them."[149] Within this space of ethos (in Heidegger's sense of a dwelling-place), Schrag states that the ethical question is "a question about the *fitting response* of the decentered subject in its encounter with the discourse and practices of the other against a backdrop of the delivered tradition."[150] Somewhat complementary to Lyotard's requirement that the participant in prescriptive language games has an obligation to listen before responding, Schrag states that the "proximity of the *ethos* of our communicative praxis," which the decentered subject shares with the other, "directs us to the requirement of *responsiveness*."[151] For Schrag, then, given the absence of an ahistorical foundation, the ground of discourse and action is ethical, and thereby, "the other" is rendered the object of knowledge.

Interpretation, Community, and Politics

Schrag's accommodation of postmodern critique within the tradition of liberal learning and reliance on a neo-humanist ethos reflects a general shortcoming of his approach. Transversal reason tends to be simply a restatement of postmodernism in positive terms rather than a project that revises, and thereby makes, postmodernist claims positive. Schrag's notion that transversal reason moves "in the space between" modernism and postmodernism is symptomatic of this problem. Schrag is only assuming that there is such a space, metaphorical or otherwise; without providing this intuitive notion with theoretical substance, it lingers as at best an aesthetically appealing image rather than what it tentatively purports to be, a reconciliation of sorts between modernity and postmodernity.[152] Transversal reason glosses over, and thus unjustifiably pacifies, the sharp philosophical contrasts that exist between modern and postmodern thought.

In particular, transversal reason does not deal directly with power and conflict as they are implicated in the activity of coming to know. While Schrag acknowledges the presence of these themes in postmodern critique, and while he recognizes that power is at play in the legitimation of knowledge in the university, his notion of transversal reason never really confronts it.[153] Schrag only briefly notes that the achievement of shared understanding across forms of life is a "hard struggle" and that "the conventions of our thought and action are tested and contested and become subject to assessment and evaluation."[154] At one point, he states that recognition of the fact that both theory and practice are context-dependent provides "a sheet anchor against any privileging of beliefs over actions, and vice versa"; in another place, he simply notes that "dissensus figures in every occasion of consensus."[155] It is not clear how, amid the flux of conflicting social practices and beliefs, the community, whether one means scholars or the general public, is ever really significantly challenged by new, controversial ideas. Yet, Schrag's term of "radical hermeneutics" suggests that inquiries that dissent from prevailing norms of the university and the general public are not liable to be easily influential. The connection between the inquirer who is engaged in intellectual activity in which received ideas are used to create divergent lines of inquiry, and the role of these inquiries relative to the social good, needs elaboration that recognizes the political aspects of inquiry and a more affirmative role for the inquirer in this regard.

Further, alien forms of thought are not easily heard and received. It is not at all self-evident that liberal learning includes an openness to alien discourse. In fact, much of the conflict in the contemporary university seems to reflect the situation that both those in power and those aspiring to power do not want to know each other and seem to advance ideas of knowledge and human society that are mutually adverse. Schrag, then, leaves a question that complements the one that emerged from my analysis of Rorty, about the explicit connection of the inquirer to the structure of society. Although the relation between the individual inquirer and the community is developed more substantially by Schrag than Rorty, it remains insufficient because it does not adequately address the political aspects of inquiry that deviate from norms.

The ideas of transversal reason and communicative praxis are not distinctive enough as the basis for a new concept of rationality. In developing these ideas, Schrag relies too heavily on modern hermeneutics, especially Heidegger and Gadamer. As a result, the idea of interpretation that Schrag proposes does not provide a basis for inquiry that is sufficiently postmodern, given the emphasis that he places on the critiques of modern inquiry by Lyotard and Rorty.

Like the analyses of those critiques earlier in this chapter, this analysis of Schrag suggests an idea of inquiry that emphasizes intellectual activity in which the aim is to experience and create new lines of inquiry. Schrag's chief contribution to an alternative idea of inquiry is that reason would be oriented toward making interpretations of established knowledge in some unconventional way. In particular, knowledge would be construed as interpretation that emerges from within the activity of inquiry, rather than being something that, while discovered "within" inquiry, nonetheless refers essentially to something that exists outside it.

The significance of transversal reason for an alternative idea of inquiry is that it emphasizes reason as being highly fluid and adaptive to different contexts, rather than being something immutable and universal that moderates new ideas. The idea of communicative practice emphasizes that the movement from abnormal to normal inquiry is a communicative activity in which interpretation, and thus creation of new ideas, does not cease with the production of a result that is then reported and received intact. Instead, the results of inquiry are offered for further interpretation, as the basis for new inquiries.

Knowledge would be something that is used by intellect to engage in activity in which value, rather than facts, is added to human experience. The aim is to create new possibilities for what it means to engage in an inquiry, thereby enhancing the capacity of the community of scholars to make a difference in reality. Thus, the idea of knowledge is tied to the idea of inquiry as an interpretive, communal activity. However, it is necessary to confront the conflict between established ideas of the community, on one hand, and ideas that challenge them, on the other. If this aspect of postmodern thought is not addressed, then it would be susceptible to the commonly made charge that it is a "neoconservative" retreat of intellect from politics. From this aspect of postmodern thought, it is possible that a meaning of "interpretation" that is distinctive can be achieved.

NOTES

1. Jean-Francois Lyotard, "Answering the Question: What is Postmodernism?," in *The Postmodern Condition: A Report on Knowledge*, trans. Geoffrey Bennington and Brian Massumi (Minneapolis: University of Minnesota Press, 1984), 79. Other work of Lyotard's where one can find less developed aspects of the theme of this book include *Political Writings*, trans. Bill Readings and Kevin Paul Geiman (Minneapolis: University of Minnesota Press, 1993); *The Postmodern Explained: Correspondence 1982–1985*, ed. Julian Pefanis and Morgan Thomas (Minneapolis: University of Minnesota Press, 1993); *The Inhuman: Reflections on Time*, trans. Geoffrey Bennington and Rachel Bowlby (Cambridge, U. K.: Polity Press, 1991); and *The Lyotard Reader*, ed. Andrew Benjamin (Oxford: Basil Blackwell, 1989).
2. *Postmodern Condition*, 15.
3. Ibid., 10.
4. Ibid., 18.
5. Ibid., 8.
6. Ibid., 28.
7. Ibid., 23.

8. Ibid., 28–29.
9. Ibid., 31–32.
10. Ibid., 36.
11. Ibid., 40.
12. Ibid., 32–33.
13. Ibid., 34–35. More precisely, in Hegelian terms, science legitimizes itself through the historical unfolding of speculative reason, or knowledge of the Spirit. In the course of this story, the people and the State are indirectly legitimized, as embodiments of Spirit.
14. Ibid., 38–39.
15. Ibid., 41–43.
16. Ibid.
17. Ibid., 60.
18. Thomas S. Kuhn, *The Structure of Scientific Revolutions*, 2d ed. enl. (Chicago: University of Chicago Press, 1970, first published, 1962).
19. Lyotard, *Postmodern Condition*, 57.
20. Ibid., 59.
21. Ibid., 44–45.
22. Ibid., 46.
23. Ibid., xxiv, 8.
24. Ibid., 50.
25. Ibid., 38.
26. Ibid., 48.
27. Ibid., 51.
28. Ibid., 53.
29. "Answering the Question: What is Postmodernism?," in *Postmodern Condition*, 81.
30. *Postmodern Condition*, 62–63.
31. Ibid., 13–15.
32. Jean-Francois Lyotard and Jean-Loup Thebaud, *Just Gaming*, trans. Wlad Godzich (Minneapolis: University of Minnesota Press, 1985), 61.
33. *Postmodern Condition*, 13–15.
34. Ibid., 43.
35. Ibid., 8.
36. *Just Gaming*, 25.
37. Ibid., 28–29.
38. Ibid., 50–53; *Postmodern Condition*, 52–53.
39. Ibid., 18–19.
40. "Answering the Question: What is Postmodernism?," in *Postmodern Condition*, 79.
41. *Just Gaming*, 14, 61.
42. Ibid., 60, 6.
43. Ibid., 66.
44. Ibid., 98.
45. *Postmodern Condition*, 15.
46. Ibid., 17.
47. *Just Gaming*, 100.
48. Ibid., 59.
49. Ibid., 50–53; *Postmodern Condition*, 52–53.
50. *Postmodern Condition*, 53.

51. Ibid., xxv.
52. *Just Gaming*, 43, 48.
53. *Postmodern Condition*, 30.
54. Ibid., 65.
55. Ibid., 66.
56. Ibid., 61.
57. Ibid., 66.
58. Richard Rorty, *Philosophy and the Mirror of Nature* (Princeton: Princeton University Press, 1979), 11. Initial development of the theme of this book can be found in Rorty's *Consequences of Pragmatism (Essays: 1972–1980)* (Minneapolis: University of Minnesota Press, 1982). See also the collection of essays in Rorty's *Objectivity, Relativism, and Truth: Philosophical Papers, vol. 1* (New York: Cambridge University Press, 1991). Rorty explores his ideas in analysis of works of literature in *Contingency, Irony, and Solidarity* (New York: Cambridge University Press, 1989). For a collection of essays by analytic philosophers that critique *Philosophy and the Mirror of Nature*, see Alan R. Malachowski, ed., *Reading Rorty: Critical Responses to* Philosophy and the Mirror of Nature *(and Beyond)* (Oxford, U. K.: Basil Blackwell, 1990). A recent book on Richard Rorty and liberal education is Rene V. Arcilla's *For the Love of Perfection: Richard Rorty and Liberal Education* (New York: Routledge, 1995). A recent book that treats Rorty in depth is David L. Hall's *Richard Rorty: Prophet and Poet of the New Pragmatism* (Albany: State University of New York Press, 1994). A good summation of Rorty's pragmatism is Konstantin Kolenda's *Rorty's Humanistic Pragmatism: Philosophy Democratized* (Tampa: University of South Florida Press, 1990).
59. Richard Rorty, "Habermas and Lyotard on Postmodernity," in *Habermas and Modernity*, ed. Richard Bernstein (Cambridge, Mass.: MIT Press, 1985), 173.
60. Ibid., 174–175.
61. *Mirror of Nature*, 31, 149.
62. Ibid., 40–41, 51–52.
63. Ibid., 45, 51–52, 62.
64. Ibid., 48–50, 140–155.
65. Ibid., 48.
66. Ibid., 3, 6, 132, 136, 152.
67. Ibid., chap. 5, chap. 6, 7, 8, 9.
68. Ibid., 318–319.
69. Ibid., 159.
70. Ibid., 358–359.
71. Ibid., 156, 157, 159.
72. Ibid., 159, 210.
73. Ibid., 303.
74. Ibid., 389.
75. Ibid., 318.
76. Ibid., 319.
77. Ibid., 320.
78. Ibid., 387.
79. Ibid., 321–322, 328–333, 335–339, 344, 363–365.
80. Ibid., 331.
81. Ibid., 356.
82. Ibid., 359.

83. Ibid., 357–365, 359.
84. Ibid., 359.
85. Ibid., 360.
86. Ibid., 362.
87. Ibid., 361.
88. Ibid., 365–366.
89. Ibid., 372.
90. Ibid., 389.
91. Ibid., 379.
92. Richard Rorty, *Essays on Heidegger and Others: Philosophical Papers, Volume 2* (New York: Cambridge University Press, 1991), 9.
93. Ibid.
94. Ibid., 3.
95. Ibid.
96. Ibid., 5.
97. Rorty has not yet done the very thing that he says philosophers should do, namely, create abnormal discourse. Yet he criticizes those Continental theorists who do that very thing, such as Lyotard, Michel Foucault, and Jacques Derrida, on the basis that they are advancing "essentialist" ideas. *Heidegger and Others*, part II.
98. Ibid., 17.
99. Ibid.
100. John Dewey, *Experience and Education* (New York: Collier-Macmillan, 1963, first published 1938).
101. *Mirror of Nature*, 366.
102. Richard Rorty, "Education, Socialization, and Individuation," *Liberal Education* 75, no. 4 (September/October 1989): 2–3.
103. Ibid.
104. Calvin O. Schrag, *The Resources of Rationality: A Response to the Postmodern Challenge* (Bloomington: University of Indiana Press, 1992), 8. Other work of Schrag's that leads up to this book includes an essay, "Rationality Between Modernity and Postmodernity," in Stephen K. White, ed., *Lifeworld and Politics: Between Modernity and Postmodernity* (Notre Dame: University of Notre Dame Press, 1989), and two books, *Communicative Praxis and the Space of Subjectivity* (Bloomington: Indiana University Press, 1986) and *Radical Reflection and the Origin of the Human Sciences* (West Lafayette: Purdue University Press, 1980). A collection of papers selected by Schrag that span the evolution of his thought over many years has recently been published. *Philosophical Papers: Betwixt and Between* (Albany: State University of New York Press, 1994).
105. *Resources of Rationality*, ix.
106. Ibid., 24, 161, 164.
107. Ibid., 97–100.
108. Ibid., 164.
109. Ibid., 9.
110. Ibid., 151–152.
111. Ibid., 158.
112. Ibid., 7, 9.
113. Ibid., 174.
114. Ibid., 151.

115. Ibid., 166.
116. Ibid., 152, 164.
117. This concept was developed by Schrag in a previous work, *Communicative Praxis and the Space of Subjectivity* (Bloomington: Indiana University Press, 1986).
118. Ibid., 6.
119. Ibid., chap. 6, chap. 7. The notion of the de-centered self does not originate with Schrag, but is a common claim among the French postmodernists.
120. *Resources of Rationality*, 58.
121. Ibid., 74–75.
122. Ibid., 61–65.
123. Ibid., 60.
124. Ibid., 72, 88, 90–91.
125. Ibid., 93.
126. Ibid., 110–11.
127. Ibid., 94.
128. Ibid., 154.
129. Ibid., 158.
130. Ibid., 166.
131. Ibid., 76.
132. Ibid., 136.
133. Ibid.
134. Ibid., 137–142.
135. Ibid., 170.
136. Ibid., 158–159.
137. Ibid., 134.
138. Ibid., 173.
139. Ibid., 173.
140. Ibid., 147, 154.
141. Ibid., 148.
142. Ibid., 148, 152–154.
143. Ibid., 148, 156.
144. Ibid., 101–102.
145. Calvin O. Schrag, "Liberal Learning in the Postmodern World," *The Key Reporter* 54, no. 1 (Autumn 1988): 3.
146. Ibid.
147. Ibid.
148. Ibid., 4.
149. Ibid.
150. *Communicative Praxis*, chap. 10.
151. Ibid., 202.
152. Ibid., 200–202.
153. Ibid., 204.
154. Throughout *Resources*, Schrag refers to the postmodern notion of "play" that is left by the alleged undecidable opposition between pairs of philosophical concepts. In essence, what he seems to be doing with the modernism/postmodernism dichotomy, albeit implicitly, is to use Jacques Derrida's claim that the search for metaphysical origins is forever deferred by the irresolvable "play" of opposing signifiers within language, as the basis for a resolution, or perhaps better, a mediation, between modern-

ism and postmodernism in the context of ongoing social practice. I explain Derrida's claim in Chapter 4. Cf. Jacques Derrida, *Of Grammatology*, trans. Gayatri Chakravorty Spivak (Baltimore: Johns Hopkins University Press, 1976).

155. *Resources of Rationality*, 35–42, 126–127; "Liberal Learning in the Postmodern World," 3.

4

Foucault and Derrida: Inquiry as Intellectual Activity that Acts Upon and Changes Reality

FOUCAULT: POLITICAL INQUIRY

> We should abandon a whole tradition that allows us to imagine that knowledge exists only where the power relations are suspended and that knowledge can only develop outside its injunctions, its demands and its interests.[1]

As with Lyotard's critique, an understanding of the implications of the late Michel Foucault's critique of progress for an alternative idea of inquiry requires an explanation of Foucault's claims about knowledge as a social phenomenon. I will first discuss his notion of power and its relationship to knowledge. This analysis will emphasize the notion of the human subject in his critique of progress. I will then describe the social role of the human sciences, which is the particular focus of Foucault's critique, and the theoretical problems that he alleges to exist in the idea of the human sciences. Finally, I will analyze the implications of his critique of knowledge for an alternative idea of inquiry.

Critique of Progress: Knowledge and Power

When Foucault uses the term "power," he does not mean ethnic, social, or religious domination, or economic exploitation.[2] While he acknowledges that these forms of group-affiliated domination and exploitation have been prevalent in different historical periods, Foucault claims that the most significant manifestation of power in Western society since the late eighteenth century "applies itself to immediate everyday life which categorizes the individual, marks him by his own individuality, attaches him to his own identity, imposes a law of truth on him which he must recognize and which others have to recognize in him. It is a form of power which makes individuals subjects."[3]

This form of power is not simply tantamount to the effects of state or rational-bureaucratic hegemony. The power relations he has in mind are not structural in this sense but are "rooted deep in the social nexus."[4] This power, moreover, is not solely a function of institutions; while institutions represent one important manifestation of power, they are not "the fundamental point of anchorage" of power relationships. Rather, power emerges basically "from the starting points of local conditions and particular needs."[5] Nor is power understood as a dichotomous relationship "between those who exclusively possess and retain it, and those who do not have it and submit to it."[6] Further, power is not an objective thing or force. Power is a social phenomenon that is always specific and local.[7] It is "a productive network which runs through the whole social body," understood in terms of concrete practices.[8] However, power is not, in itself, violence. It is "a way of acting upon an acting subject or acting subjects by virtue of their acting or being capable of action."[9]

Specifically, "power is exercised only over free subjects . . . individual or collective subjects who are faced with a field of possibilities in which several ways of behaving, several reactions and diverse comportments may be realized."[10] A key aspect of power in modernity is its relationship to the human beings as individuals. According to Foucault, the modern concept and understanding of the human being as an individual reflects that the individual is the focal object, vehicle, and effect of power.[11] "The individual is not a pre-given entity which is seized on by the exercise of power. The individual, with his identity and characteristics, is the product of a relation of power exercised over bodies, multiplicities, movements, desires, forces."[12]

Knowledge and power imply each other, though they are not identical. "We are subjected to the production of truth through power and we cannot exercise power except through the production of truth. This is the case in every society, but I believe that in ours . . . we are forced to produce the truth of power that our society demands, of which it has need, in order to function: we *must* speak the truth; we are constrained or condemned to confess or to discover the truth."[13] Truth is understood by Foucault in terms of this relation between knowledge and power. Specifically, truth is "an ensemble of rules according to which the true and the false are separated and specific effects of power attached to the true."[14]

One of Foucault's most controversial claims is that since their inception the discourses of the human sciences have been instrumental in the production of subjects through the exercise of power. He argues that the rise of the scientific study of the human being in modernity is associated with the appearance of what Foucault calls "disciplinary technologies," or "procedures which allowed the effects of power to circulate in a manner at once continuous, uninterrupted, adapted and individualised throughout the entire social body."[15] Foucault claims that disciplinary technologies emerged, beginning in the seventeenth century but not becoming prominent until the nineteenth, as organized means for the purpose of making human beings productive, cooperative participants in society: individuals whose behavior "consolidated the system and contributed to its overall functioning."[16]

The human body, as the ultimate local site on which power is concentrated, is a prominent element in Foucault's notion of disciplinary technologies and his critique of the human subject. The human body serves as the target of disciplinary technology, the object by which the human being is manipulated into acknowledging itself as a "docile, productive subject." In the nineteenth century:

> an art of the human body was born, which was directed not only at the growth of its skills, nor at the intensification of its subjection, but at the formation of a relation that in the mechanism itself makes it more obedient as it becomes more useful, and conversely. What was then being formed was a policy of coercions that act upon the body, a calculated manipulation of its elements, its gestures, its behaviour.[17]

The individual human body is not simply known: it is acted upon. The presence of the body means that the human being, including the intellectual who pursues knowledge, is capable of being adversely affected by practice. If it did not have this capacity, this vulnerability, the human body would not be the strategic object by which human beings have been, according to Foucault, coerced into becoming "free" subjects.

Disciplinary technologies are practical (not essentially ideological or institutional) techniques and procedures that act as mechanisms of power because they are "economically advantageous and politically useful."[18] They proceed by directing various techniques upon the object of the human body; in this process, human subjects are invested with individuality. These techniques involve four basic dimensions:[19] (1) the efficient distribution and circulation of individuals in "cells, places, and ranks" according to the precise analysis of space; (2) the control of activities; (3) the organization of time in profitable durations; (4) and the creation of productive forces "superior to the sum of elementary forces that composed it."[20]

The creation and production of certain kinds of knowledge is a key element in the operation of disciplinary technologies.[21] According to Foucault, this knowledge, the human sciences, makes possible methods of observation, techniques of registration, procedures for investigation and research, and apparatuses of control.[22] Power is exercised through "these subtle mechanisms." "And this investigation enables us to rediscover one of the conditions of the emergence of the human sciences: the great nineteenth-century effort in discipline and normalisation."[23]

Critique of Progress: The Human Sciences and the Individual Subject

For Foucault, an understanding of the social construction of knowledge in the human sciences is concerned with knowledge as an instrument of power in the rise of organized, rational-bureaucratic European society.[24] However, the emphasis Foucault places on power in his historical analysis of it has led many commentators to believe that power is his primary concern. Foucault himself asserts that his primary object of study is the historical phenomenon of the human subject, not power. "My objective, instead, has been to create a history of the different modes by which, in our culture, human beings are made subjects," and these modes are uses of power.[25]

In his earlier work, before he explicitly developed his concept of power, Foucault analyzes the constitution of human beings as objects of study in the human sciences through what he calls "dividing practices." For example, he claims that the description of people as mentally ill or physically ill and their "internment" in asylums or hospitals are means by which the modern human subject seeks to cleanse itself of "the other" within itself.[26] Subsequently, he examined the emergence of discourse regarding sexuality and the self in the constitution and control of human subjects.[27] In all of these cases, the role of knowledge in the human sciences is identified as a key element in the proliferation of disciplinary technologies in the nineteenth century. A prominent example is the formation and growth of psychology:

It was the emergence . . . of a new type of the supervision—both knowledge and power—over individuals who resisted disciplinary normalization . . . the supervision of normality was firmly encased in a medicine or a psychiatry that provided it with a sort of "scientificity" . . . marked a new era.[28]

Foucault identifies, by historical (or more accurately, what he calls "archaeological") analysis, alleged theoretical shortcomings of the human sciences that, he claims, are fatal to the idea that they are justified as autonomous realms of scientific knowledge.[29] Like Lyotard, Foucault subordinates epistemological argument to a historical analysis that is predicated on the social contingency of the scientific pursuit of knowledge; in this case, it is the creation of the human sciences as "discourse that takes as its object man as an empirical entity."[30]

Foucault argues that when the human being became an object of modern study in the nineteenth century, it could not be simply cast as an external object like other entities because it was both subject and object.[31] He claims that the epistemological problem of the human sciences is that "representation is not simply an object for the human sciences; it is . . . the very field upon which the human sciences occur."[32] Thus, the human sciences "find themselves treating as their object what is in fact their condition of possibility. . . . They proceed from that which is given to representation to that which renders representation possible, but which is still representation."[33]

The problem is that unlike other objects of knowledge, since the human being is, for the human sciences, both subject and object, knower and known, it cannot be objectively represented like other entities, yet historically the human sciences "have been unable to find a way around the primacy of representation."[34] In essence, Foucault is claiming that the human sciences, like the natural sciences, rely on representation, yet representation as a form of knowledge is insufficient to know the human knower, because in this case, the human knower is both object and subject, which defies the idea of objective knowledge.[35] As soon as the knower seeks to know itself, it is no longer a knower, at least in the way that scholars in the human sciences have generally aspired, namely, a scientific model of inquiry and knowledge.

Foucault is not claiming that the sole purpose of the production of knowledge in the human sciences has been or is to create productive individual subjects. Similarly, he is not arguing that the human sciences are simply, or necessarily, an extension of disciplinary technologies.[36] He is, however, arguing that the human sciences are historically situated within a profoundly altered foundation of knowledge (what the early Foucault calls an *episteme*, and later, a *dispositef*) that emerged in response to the strategic need for a discourse to ground the organization of modern society as a collective of disciplined, productive individual "subjects."[37] In *Discipline and Punish*, the first book in which he articulates his notion of power, Foucault makes this point in reference to one of the alleged "armatures" of power and knowledge that he claims to identify, in this case the establishment of correctional prisons in the nineteenth century:

I am not saying that the human sciences emerged from the prison. But, if they have been able to be formed and to produce so many profound changes in the episteme, it is because they have been conveyed by a specific and new modality of power: a certain policy of the body, a certain way of rendering the group of men docile and useful. . . . Knowable man . . . is the object-effect of this analytical investment, of this domination-observation.[38]

While the example of prisons is his most extensive illustration of sites where disciplinary technologies and the "power-knowledge" of the human sciences are focused, Foucault details a number of other examples, including factories, schools, hospitals, and the military.

The Politics of Inquiry

According to Foucault, then, the pursuit of knowledge, especially knowledge of the human being, rather than being an intellectual counter to power, has in modern history played a significant role in the complex utilization of power. This position does not mean that Foucault categorically rejects the idea of scientifically demonstrable knowledge.[39] Nor does it mean that the relationship between the pursuit of knowledge and power, or the results that this relationship has produced, are *only* harmful. Foucault is interested in the historical relationship between the rise and growth of the human sciences and concepts, on the one hand, and the emergence and development of organized practices, processes, and techniques that created, classified, and controlled individuals in dichotomous categories such as normal/abnormal, healthy/diseased, worker/vagrant, and citizen/criminal on the other.

Thus, Foucault's primary goal is not to offer an alternative historical account of the ways that the pursuit of knowledge of human beings has been a cornerstone of the systematic determination of the individual. He is interested in not only understanding how, and for what ends, the idea of the human subject has been formed and put into practice by the production of knowledge in modernity. His goal is to change the present by transforming the way that human beings think about and act upon themselves and each other.

He is particularly interested in the implications of his critique for the role of inquirer in society. Foucault argues that these implications are essentially political, since "'Truth' is linked in a circular relation with systems of power which produce and sustain it, and to effects of power which it induces and which extend it."[40] However, although the definition and production of knowledge are implicated in the movement of power, the problem that Foucault raises for an alternative idea of inquiry is not a problem of how to extricate the pursuit of knowledge from the articulation of power. To think that they are opposed is part of the ruse by which intellectuals are manipulated into perpetuating totalization. For Foucault, theory is unavoidably political.

Intellectuals are themselves agents of this system of power—the idea of their responsibility for "consciousness" and discourse forms part of the system. The intellectual's role is no longer to place himself "somewhat ahead and to the side" in order to express the stifled truth of the collectivity; rather, it is to struggle against the forms of power that transform him into its object and instrument in the sphere of "knowledge," "truth," "consciousness," and "discourse."[41]

Thus, Foucault wants to change the ways that intellectuals function presently in the circle of "knowledge-power." The political problem for the contemporary community of intellectuals is, then, "the political, economic, institutional regime of the production of truth" that their social location in institutions of higher education helps to maintain.[42]

The emphasis on power in the creation of the modern idea of the human individual, in whatever version, reflects that Foucault is profoundly concerned with the totalizing effects of systematically organized modern social life on human beings. He claims that modern political notions like freedom and liberation are, at least historically, prerequisites of, rather than responses to, totalization.[43] Similarly, freedom of inquiry and the associations of this idea with aims such as democracy and humanity would be subject to this critique. Like Lyotard, Foucault is especially concerned with the totalization of individual human beings by the manipulation and complicity of intellectuals in the production of knowledge for the sake of the social system, and the university as an institution of totalization of intellectuals.

Finally, all these present struggles revolve around the question: Who are we? They are a refusal of these abstractions, of economic and ideological state violence which ignore who we are individually, and also a refusal of a scientific or administrative inquisition which determines who one is.[44]

In order to serve the social good, the problem for the intellectual is not simply to change how others think, but to change the ways that people act as well. According to Foucault, to pursue this end, the inquirer cannot stand off to the side of the community and produce knowledge with the hope that it will influence others to act. To do so is to perpetuate a social role that pacifies intellect for the sake of the socioeconomic system. Instead, the inquirer must aim to change the ensemble of rules that determine what is true and what is false, and that thereby govern action. Foucault is attempting to move intellect from ideas to action, from thinking about to acting upon reality.

Inquiry Acts Upon Reality

Foucault's concept of power, since it emphasizes the practical, local effects of power and the proximity of inquiry to the activities, behavior, and thoughts of individuals and groups outside of the university, is consistent with the critiques of progress examined in the previous chapter. On one level, Foucault's critique contributes a focus on the political aspects of the inquirer and inquiry, and the political responsibility of the inquirer and the university for not only the uses of knowledge, but for its construction as well.

However, the implications of his critique for an alternative idea of inquiry are not limited to these political aspects. In a general sense, Foucault is seeking to change the present by changing the past. His approach is to take well-established social institutions such as hospitals and prisons, whose reason for existence and basic functions are generally taken for granted, and make them into essentially new objects of inquiry. The beginning point for this kind of inquiry is to think of familiar objects of knowledge and action as utterly unfamiliar, and to ask how they came about. Implicitly, this approach assumes that the existence of these institutions, and of the practices that they support, may not have emerged "normally," that is, consistent with the ways that we normally think about the purposes of these institutions. To take Foucault's approach is to place these practices and institutions in an entirely new context. In Rorty's terms, Foucault renders them abnormal, or un-normalizes them.

I believe that the problem does not consist in drawing the line between that in a discourse which falls under the category of scientificity or truth, and that which comes under some other category, but in seeing historically how effects of truth are produced within discourses which in themselves are neither true nor false.[45]

Further, this approach is asking the question of how reality is constituted *by inquiry*. It is not simply the products of inquiry, but the activity of inquiry that is crucial in the formation and maintenance of these institutions and practices.

Foucault's concept of "knowledge-power" can be understood as emphasizing an idea of inquiry in which knowledge does not stand alone from inquiry as something to be transmitted and applied; rather, it implies an idea of inquiry as an activity that involves working with knowledge to make a new reality in the course of inquiry. Inquiry in this sense is an endeavor that acts upon reality, and knowledge is that which is acted with, thus changing reality in some way specific to that particular inquiry.

This idea of inquiry provides a distinctive idea of interpretation that was lacking in Schrag's critique. Inquiry is an intellectual activity in which the aim is to change the present by reinterpreting the past. The connection of this aim with the community is that the inquirer aims to change how others perceive and how others act. In Foucault's own case, the aim is to create a history that accomplishes this end: "One 'fictions' history starting from a political reality that renders it true, one 'fictions' a politics that does not yet exist starting from a historical truth."[46]

Thus, the purpose of engaging in an inquiry is not to challenge "normal" accounts. Nor is it to get the "right" historical account. Rather, the interpreter acts upon established knowledge in order to change reality beyond changing how it is normally perceived. However, even if political and historical aspects are involved in any inquiry, they do not wholly define it. Foucault leaves the question of what the idea of acting upon reality, and the idea of working with knowledge, mean in a general sense. If they mean changing reality in some way that is not limited to changing ideas, then an alternative concept of inquiry that is influenced by Foucault's critique would need to explain more fully the nature of these other kinds of changes. It would also have to explain what is meant by changing reality in ways that go beyond changing perceptions of reality.

DERRIDA: CRITICAL INQUIRY

> From the pre-Socratics to Heidegger . . . the history of truth, the truth of truth, has always been . . . the debasement of writing, and its repression outside "full" speech.[47]

For Jacques Derrida, any philosophical text that attempts to describe, explain, and defend a theory of truth, or to make a knowledge-claim, unjustifiably invokes what he calls a "metaphysics of presence." Derrida claims that the idea of truth cannot be justified because it is necessarily subject to a fundamental problematic relation. He reveals this alleged problematic in "deconstructive" readings of important philosophical texts. Derrida asserts that a specific problematic relation emerges regardless of whether the foundation of knowledge that is implicitly assumed, or explicitly advanced, in a given text is objective reality, an autonomous or transcendental subject, natural or human history, or empirical or logical-deductive science.

While the English translations of Derrida's work have used the words "presence" and "self-presence," a more illuminating expression of what Derrida means is that which absolutely is, especially in the sense of an absolute as it is presently accessible to human reason.[48] Derrida claims that this idea of absolute presence is always implicated whenever the idea of knowledge as something pure or whole, something unblemished by uncertainty, is relied upon in a text. At one level, Derrida is alleging that the notion of knowledge as ultimately knowledge of something absolute or universal is a cultural construct rather than an accurate description of the nature of things. However, for Derrida, knowledge is not simply one cultural construct among others. He attempts to demonstrate, on the basis of intensive textual analysis, that the idea of absolute presence contains a necessary problematic that effectively renders the idea an illusion. Derrida believes that the implications of his critique render problematic the intellectual fabric of Western civilization.

Although he uses the term "metaphysics of presence" to describe the basic target of his critique, Derrida's work cannot be simply confined to a "Continental" approach. Like Rorty, Derrida believes that the human's basic dependence on language to signify and communicate meaning in thought and experience carries with it insurmountable problems for those humans who pursue certain knowledge of reality. Whereas Rorty uses the terms epistemology and ontology to critique the Anglo-American analytic tradition, Derrida, being of a different philosophical tradition, writes of metaphysics. Further, while he writes from within the so-called Continental tradition, Derrida, like Rorty, intends his critique to have significance beyond his philosophical tradition.

Unlike Rorty, however, Derrida is not aiming essentially at the academic tradition of philosophy. Although philosophy is his primary means, he assumes that philosophical ideas are ideas that, while originating as intellectual concerns in the thought of ancient Greek philosophers, permeate Western thought in general. It is these ideas, rather than philosophy per se, that Derrida is most concerned with. Moreover, Derrida asserts that ordinary language is the language of Western metaphysics.[49] Thus, he means to make a much broader statement than does Rorty. Even a summation of this complicated, and rather elliptical, argument requires some carefully chosen detail. After analyzing the key elements of Derrida's position, I will delve into the implications of his position for the meaning of inquiry.

Critique of Progress: Speech, Writing, and Truth

Derrida's argument begins with the position that philosophers of the Western epoch, from the time of ancient Greece across modernity, have been concerned with the status of speech and writing relative to the idea of truth.[50] A basic claim that he makes is that across Western intellectual history, speech has been accorded a superior status to writing on the basis that speech is a natural medium.[51] Further, Derrida claims that the conventional idea of signification, and thus knowledge of reality, has always been predicated on the idea of truth as presence that is revealed by pure speech.

Human speech is thought to be "natural," he claims, because it is the product of the authentic human voice. Since the vocal chords are a part of the human being, and since the human voice (including one's "inner voice") expresses a human thought at virtually the same moment that the human forms the thought, speech has typically held a special status as a signifier of knowledge in the minds of philosophers and writers. Speech is a signifier that is directly connected with, or present to, human thought. As such, speech is the natural means by which intellectual experience of reality is manifested; speech is so close to that actual experience that it is discrepant by a breath from presence.[52] Thus, speech has a natural bond to thought that apprehends reality: it affords the human the capacity to pronounce, within itself and to others, the realization of knowledge nearly coincident with the moment of its realization in the mind. To be a knower is to speak the truth.

In contrast, graphic writing is twice removed from human cognition: it is a signifier and it is exterior to, and wholly separate from, the mind. Writing has been relegated to an inferior role because it signifies a signifier that is allegedly closer to presence, namely, the human voice.[53] That which is written is an artifact outside thought, whereas speech is naturally bonded to thought. Writing is tainted by its deviation from human intellect. Being a signifier on the page instead of interior to the knower, writing is liable to depart from knowledge of reality.[54]

Derrida is struck by the lengths that many philosophers go to make a sharp distinction between writing and speech. He places particular importance in their alleged general tendency to assign writing a grossly inferior place relative to speech as a signifier of knowledge of reality, to the point that writing is sometimes characterized as evil and impure. In his readings of Plato, Rousseau, Kant, Hegel, Husserl, Heidegger, and many others, Derrida claims to reveal their attempts to insulate, and thereby purify, speech as the natural signifier that is intimate with reality. Most importantly, Derrida's intricate analysis of their texts purports to demonstrate that, far from succeeding in "drawing" this distinction, these thinkers are unable to avoid using metaphors derived from writing in order to have human speech manifest knowledge of reality.

For Derrida, the implications of this alleged problematic are profound. The apparently inescapable infiltration of the idea of writing into the idea of speech (and vice versa) is not a large-scale linguistic or logical error that can be cleaned up by analytic reason. Rather, it is a paradox of signification that renders the idea of knowledge, where "knowledge" is the signification of that which is essentially present to a properly attuned mind, illusory.[55]

Derrida argues that the unjustified superiority of speech over writing reached a new zenith with the advent of modern philosophy. This occurred when knowledge became articulated as "self-presence," that is, as presence that is revealed to an attentive and clear-minded knower or subject.[56] To understand the basis for Derrida's claim that this relation is inherently problematic, one must understand the implications that he derives from some principles of structural linguistics, especially the theoretical work of Ferdinand de Saussure. Derrida claims that the distinction that Saussure and others make between signified and signifier, as complementary elements of a unified sign, is simply a recent reiteration of the philosophical prioritization of speech over writing.[57]

Of similar importance for Derrida is Saussure's assertion that the meaning of any sign is essentially a function of how it differs from other signs. For Saussure, this claim means that for any sign, the association of a particular signifier and a particular signified is arbitrary, purely a matter of convention.

The first consequence to be drawn from this is that the signified concept is never present in itself, in an adequate presence that would refer only to itself. Every concept is necessarily and essentially inscribed in a chain or a system, within which it refers to another and to other concepts, by the systematic play of differences.[58]

Meaning for a given sign emerges as the differentiation of that sign from other signs. A sign has no intrinsic, autonomous meaning, and a signifier is not a transparent revelation of an essential signified.[59] Now, Derrida claims that within this scheme Saussure nevertheless privileged human speech as a form of signifier on the basis that speech, as the form of signifier produced by the human voice, has a natural bond with logos. In contrast, the form of signifier that is writing has "the exteriority that one attributes to utensils."[60] Most importantly, Derrida claims that Saussure is simply reiterating, in terms of modern structural linguistics, a basic tenet of Western inquiry.[61] The tradition is uncritical because it does not question the basis for its belief that writing is "a deviation from nature."[62]

It describes or rather reflects the structure of a certain type of writing: phonetic writing, which we use and within whose element the *episteme* in general (science and philosophy), and linguistics in particular, could be founded.[63]

The apex of Derrida's argument is the following. The position that assigns writing the subordinate role of graphic substitution for speech, yet claims that signs are essentially arbitrary and take on meaning by their differences, reveals something important about writing in the very attempt to minimize it. The idea signified by the word "writing" implies a human activity that is considerably broader than being simply a graphic substitution for speech. "The very idea of institution—hence of the arbitrariness of the sign—is unthinkable before the possibility of writing and outside of its horizon."[64]

Derrida is claiming here that the Saussurian notion of the arbitrariness of signs is derived from the notion, which Derrida alleges goes back at least to Socrates, that writing in its most basic sense is "inscription and especially the durable institution of a sign."[65] Therefore, argues Derrida, the traditional, narrow idea of writing, of writing as the graphic inscription of phonos at a second remove from logos, is only one case of a broader notion of writing, "writing in general," or inscription, that encompasses phonos: "speech . . . is already in itself a writing."[66] Since the essential arbitrariness of signs implies that the act of signification is a human invention, rather than an act of natural necessity, then, in a sense, human thought, language, and expression is inscription "before" it is anything else, whether the event under consideration is a speech act or some other act. Thus, goes his argument, the Western predilection that he calls "phonocentrism" and the accompanying degradation of writing to mere mimetic stand-in for speech are unjustified.

Differance

In the key essay "Differance," Derrida makes this argument directly against the position that writing is purely *graphe* or "phonetic writing":

There is no purely and strictly phonetic writing. What is called phonetic writing can only function—in principle and *de jure,* and not due to some factual and technical inadequacy—by incorporating nonphonetic "signs" (punctuation, spacing, etc.); but when we examine their structure and necessity, we will quickly see that they are ill described by the concept of signs.[67]

The idea that writing is purely an exterior mark for speech is contradicted by the fact that graphic writing requires elements, such as spacing and punctuation marks, that are not phonetic. Just as these elements serve to indicate differences between words in written text, yet convey no meaning in themselves, the difference in sound between spoken words gives spoken words meaning but conveys no meaning in itself. Most importantly, this condition, that difference in both cases is requisite for meaning but is in itself absent, or outside meaning in itself, indicates that the idea of pure presence is a fiction. Difference is both necessary for there to be meaning and a necessary condition that belies ultimate meaning.

We must be referred to an order, then, that resists philosophy's founding opposition between the sensible and the intelligible. The order that resists this opposition, that resists it because it sustains it, is designated in a movement of differance . . . *between* speech and writing.[68]

Derrida creates the word "differance" to signify this necessary condition that he claims exists, conceptually and practically, between speech and writing such that their relative priority, on the basis that one purely signifies truth, is "undecidable." In French, the "correct" spelling of the word "difference" is, like the English, with an *e*. Derrida deliberately spells the word with the letter *a* to make a rhetorical point: in French, differance is pronounced the same as difference, yet they are not identical. The distinction is "purely graphic: it is written or read, but it is not heard."[69] Thus, Derrida designates "differance" to signify his position that speech and writing mutually imply each other without resolution: they imply a "*sameness* which is not *identical*."[70]

Rather than being about knowledge of reality, differance signifies what I have called a condition that Derrida claims necessarily occurs in the effort to make basic epistemological and scientific distinctions. More specifically, by "differance," Derrida signifies two conditions that emerge in any effort to make absolute determinations.[71] I will refer to the speech/writing opposition to explain and illustrate these alleged conditions. The first condition that differance signifies is simply Saussure's claim that a sign takes on meaning by virtue of its difference from other signs: speech has meaning in terms of its difference from writing, and vice versa. The second condition is what Derrida calls "deferral." Since speech is constituted with reference to writing, speech as a full, "pure," or autonomous idea is necessarily deferred (and vice versa): there is no pure sign. The alleged necessity of these two conditions is what Derrida means by the statement that differance signifies a "sameness that is not identical."[72] "In the one case 'to differ' signifies nonidentity; in the other case it signifies the order of the *same*."[73] Speech and writing are not entirely distinct, nor are they identical.

Further, these conditions reflect there being no sharp distinction between signifier and signified. The idea of pure speech is the idea of a fully transparent, or pure, signifier, a signifier that can simply reveal reality as it absolutely is, or what Derrida calls the "transcendental signified."[74] Since writing infiltrates speech, and vice versa, there is no form of either of these signifiers that simply mirrors something that is absolutely not itself a signifier. Thus, the unit of signification, the sign, which depends on the sharp distinction between its elements, the signifier and the signified, is disorganized. With it, the foundation of signification, the idea that there is something that is not a sign, namely, that which absolutely is, is rendered problematic.

Most importantly, Derrida asserts that the condition of difference cannot be resolved: there is no Hegelian synthesis, but rather an endless "play" of opposing terms. Having found the basic condition of differance in the opposition speech/writing, Derrida, in a kind of inversion of the Cartesian generalization of clear and distinct ideas from cogito ergo sum, claims that this condition exists in many other philosophical "hierarchies" that purport to make absolute distinctions, such as good/evil, intelligible/sensible, mind/body, reason/passion, and nature/culture.

Deconstruction and General Writing

The operation Derrida calls deconstruction is a strategy by which he claims to reveal differance as a consequence of the logic of a given philosophical or literary text.[75] Deconstruction reveals differance by a so-called "double gesture." Derrida inverts the hierarchy that is claimed in a given text, by showing how the allegedly superior (in the sense of desirable, or good, or true) term presupposes, in some sense, the inferior term. What seems inferior is, in that sense, actually superior according to the logic (or illogic) of the text. He then displaces or disrupts the entire opposition on the basis that what was claimed to be purely inferior is, by the very logic of the text, partially superior.[76] In other words, displacement is the destruction of what had been alleged or implied to be a stable hierarchy. The effect is to disorganize the hierarchy of the opposition without destroying it.

Derrida is not arguing that what was thought to be essentially or naturally superior is in fact essentially or naturally inferior. Rather, he is asserting that a pure distinction, such that either term is wholly above the other term of an opposition, cannot be justified in a literal reading of a given text. Thus, he is not asserting that, for example, writing is wholly superior to speech as a form of signification. In a sense, "writing in general," or institution, is indeed superior to speech, for reasons that I have already described. Yet this superiority is incomplete: speech is partially prior to writing within the context of Derrida's reasoning.[77]

Representation mingles with what it represents, to the point where one speaks as one writes, one thinks as if the represented were nothing more than the shadow or reflection of the representer. . . . In this play of representation, the point of origin becomes ungraspable.[78]

Thus, "writing in general," like differance, is supposedly not another absolute foundation. Yet writing in general is very important to Derrida's approach to analyzing texts; sometimes he even calls it arche-writing, though he is quick to disclaim that this designation means that it is true.[79] What, then, is "writing in general," or what I have just called "the writing of differance," beyond "inscription and especially the durable institution of a sign"?[80] To answer this question, it is useful to survey a range of Derrida's responses. Derrida asserts that the word "writing" in the general sense is readily apparent in a wide variety of cultural realms of expression and action. Writing designates the elements, actions, and actors that give rise to an inscription, as well as the physical inscription itself. "All this to describe not only the system of notation secondarily connected with these activities but the essence and the content of these activities themselves."[81]

Elsewhere, Derrida states that the play of differance prevents any word or idea from being the absolute center of things.[82] He also states that writing and text are not reducible either to the sensible or visible presence of the graphic or the literal.[83] In the interview "Semiology and Grammatology," Derrida explicitly identifies the "new concept of writing" with the recognition that "no element can function as a sign without referring to another element which itself is not simply present. . . . This interweaving, this textile, is the *text* produced only in the transformation of another text."[84]

General writing is "the "generative movement in the play of differences. The latter are neither fallen from the sky nor inscribed once and for all in a closed system. . . . Differences are the effects of transformations."[85] General writing is then the engagement of differance: to engage in writing is to elicit and produce the play of differance across and between culturally given dichotomies, pillars of Western culture that, claims Derrida, do not insulate the true from the false but implicate each in the other, thereby implicating intellectual and cultural foundations. However, for Derrida, this recognition does not mean that one can simply leave the history of Western inquiry for an utterly new form.[86]

Inquiry Aims to Alter Reality

Derrida asserts that any knowledge-determination occurs only within differance: "undecidability is always a determinate oscillation between possibilities (for example, of meaning, but also of facts)."[87] For Derrida, one does not think for knowledge of reality and thereby live truthfully; rather, in living this way, one perpetuates distinctions that may harm as well as preserve and advance civilization.

This night begins to lighten a little at the moment when linearity—which is not loss or absence but the repression of pluri-dimensional symbolic thought—relaxes its oppression because it begins to sterilize the technical and scientific economy that it has long favored.[88]

Differance, "neither a foundation, nor a ground, nor an origin," is a condition that is activated whenever discourse points toward "the transcendental signified."[89] Derrida claims that Western intellectual traditions typically point in that direction. If one takes Derrida on his own terms (which his critics often resolutely and, I think, rather uncritically, refuse to do), then it would seem that the knower is stuck between undecidable theoretical oppositions.[90] These oppositions have functioned as the foundational constructs upon which the modern idea of knowledge is predicated. For Derrida, the language of knowledge of reality is circular: every signified is a signifier and vice versa. Rather than finding freedom in the pursuit of knowledge, the seeker of knowledge, the human being that speaks for logos, is stuck in the circle of logocentrism.

Yet Derrida is not spending his professional life simply negating Western theoretical foundations. He is carefully attempting to move language out of the idea of true and false, to another way of thought and discourse. "I do not believe, that someday it will be possible *simply* to escape metaphysics."[91]

Certainly a new conceptualization is to be produced, but it must take into account the fact that conceptualization itself . . . can reintroduce what one wants to "criticize." This is why this word cannot be purely "theoretical" or "conceptual" or "discursive," I mean cannot be the work of a discourse entirely regulated by essence, meaning, truth, consciousness, ideality, etc. What I call *text* is also that which "practically" inscribes and overflows the limits of such a discourse.[92]

Since any conventional inquiry involves signification of some phenomena or idea, the problem that Derrida leaves is that inquiry as it is conventionally construed is subject to the "undecidable" oscillation between signifier and signified. What new conceptualization of inquiry emerges in the wake of this critique? Derrida's notion of general writing is the most significant aspect of his critique for an alternative idea of inquiry in several related ways.

First, Derrida's critique provides content to inquiry as an activity that creates languages that deviate from normal ones, which I inferred from the critiques of Lyotard, Rorty, and Schrag. The notion of general writing as all that gives rise to an inscription, especially the essence and content of these activities themselves, clearly implies that a new conceptualization of inquiry inferred from his critique of signification would emphasize inquiry as an activity.[93] Most importantly, Derrida's focus on the "physical gesture" of general writing, and his inclusion of examples such activities as cinematography, choreography, music, sculpture, and athletics, suggests an idea of inquiry in which the activity, and the languages that are involved in the activity, are not necessarily composed of letters and words.

Second, the idea of general writing addresses several questions raised by my analysis of Foucault's critique. Derrida's notion of general writing as an activity that follows from the recognition that any knowledge-claim involves the introduction or "institution" of a sign seems to imply that the inquirer acts upon reality with the intention of changing it. The kinds of activities listed above also broaden the idea of acting upon reality, since they emphasize or require skilled physical activity, or the use of technology. Restated, Rorty's repertoire of useful tools that the inquirer would have at its disposal in the effort to create and normalize abnormal vocabularies could include other forms of expression besides the signification of reality.

Third, the idea of "durable institution" provides an alternative idea of inquiry with an outcome or product, which was lacking in the other critiques. Durable institution suggests that the change would be a tangible outcome in the form of some thing or condition that is intentionally altered or reshaped as a consequence of acting upon reality. Most importantly, this outcome could be constituted by materials other than, or in addition to, words or images that signify reality.

I have shown that in the context of inquiry, the critiques of Derrida and the other postmodern philosophers that I have examined are both fundamental and constructive. They are fundamental because they are directed at the basic idea of what it means to engage in an inquiry. They are constructive because they do not end with criticism. Instead, they explore and encourage an alternative idea of inquiry, although that alternative idea is not fully developed.

In order to develop it further, it is useful to take a step back and think about the general nature of these five critiques. The fact that each of the critiques is both fundamental and constructive suggests that they are responding to a basic condition of inquiry as it is currently comprehended and practiced by scholars in institutions of higher education. Further, since each of these critiques poses alternatives that emphasize new intellectual activities based on aims that are determined in the present, rather than reform of conventional inquiry grounded on aims pronounced in the past, it would seem that the basic condition that they are responding to acts as a significant constraint on intellect; further, that this condition has something to do with the past constraining the possibilities of intellectual activity in the present; and that there are good reasons why this constraint is not necessary or desirable.

To develop an alternative idea of inquiry in more depth, then, it is important to think about what it means to engage in a conventional or modern inquiry generally, and the basic condition of modern inquiry that acts as an unnecessary and undesirable constraint. The question that I will pursue in the next chapter is: What is the basic condition of modern inquiry in relation to the past, how does it act as a constraint on intellect, and why is this constraint unnecessary? With an answer to this question, this inquiry will be in a position to more fully develop the alternative conception that has begun to emerge.

NOTES

1. Michel Foucault, *Discipline and Punish: The Birth of the Prison*, trans. A. Sheridan (New York: Random House, 1979), 27–28. There is a large number of books on Foucault's philosophy. Probably the most widely regarded book on Foucault is Hubert L. Dreyfus and Paul Rabinow, *Michel Foucault: Beyond Structuralism and Hermeneutics* (Chicago: University of Chicago Press, 2d ed., 1983). Others of note include Gary Gutting, ed., *The Cambridge Companion to Foucault* (Cambridge, U. K.: Cambridge University Press, 1994); Todd May, *Between Genealogy and Epistemology: Psychology, Politics, and Knowledge in the Thought of Michel Foucault* (University Park: Pennsylvania State University Press, 1993); Martin Kusch, *Foucault's Strata and Fields: An Investigation into Archaeological and Genealogical Science Studies* (Dordrecht: Kluwer Academic, 1991); James W. Bernauer, *Michel Foucault's Force of Flight: Toward an Ethics for Thought* (Atlantic Highlands, N.J.: Humanities Press International, 1990); Gary Gutting, *Michel Foucault's Archaeology of Scientific Reason* (Cambridge, U. K.: Cambridge University Press, 1989); Gilles Deleuze, *Foucault* (London: Athlone, 1988); Jonathan Arac, ed., *After Foucault: Humanistic Knowledge, Postmodern Challenges* (New Brunswick, N.J.: Rutgers University Press, 1988); James Bernauer and David Rasmussen, eds., *The Final Foucault* (Cambridge, Mass.: MIT Press, 1988); Mark Cousins and Athar Hussain, *Michel Foucault* (London: Macmillan, 1984). There are two collections of essays that begin to think about some implications of Foucault's idea of power for education. Several essays implicate power in analytic philosophy, the transmission of knowledge, and the natural sciences: Chuck Dyke,

"Extralogical Excavation: Philosophy in the Age of Shovelry," Mary Schmelzer, "Panopticism and Postmodern Pedagogy," and Joseph Rouse, "Foucault and the Natural Sciences," in John Caputo and Mark Yount, eds., *Foucault and the Critique of Institutions* (University Park: Pennsylvania University Press, 1993), 101–162. A collection of essays by British educators uses power as a starting point for critiques of the allegedly oppressive nature of British public schools. Stephen J. Ball, ed., *Foucault and Education: Disciplines and Knowledge* (London: Routledge, 1990).

2. Michel Foucault, "The Subject and Power," afterword in *Beyond Structuralism and Hermeneutics*, 212.

3. Ibid.

4. Ibid., 222.

5. Michel Foucault, "The Eye of Power," in *Power/Knowledge: Selected Interviews and Other Writings*, ed. Colin Gordon (New York: Random House, 1980), 159.

6. Foucault, "Two Lectures," in *Power/Knowledge*, 98.

7. "The Subject and Power," in *Beyond Structuralism and Hermeneutics*, 219.

8. Foucault, "Truth and Power," in *Power/Knowledge*, 119, and "Two Lectures," in *Power/Knowledge*, 97.

9. "The Subject and Power," in *Beyond Structuralism and Hermeneutics*, 220.

10. Ibid., 221.

11. "Two Lectures," in *Power/Knowledge*, 98.

12. Foucault, "Questions on Geography," in *Power/Knowledge*, 73–74.

13. "Two Lectures," in *Power/Knowledge*, 93.

14. "Truth and Power," in *Power/Knowledge*, 132.

15. Ibid., 119.

16. "Two Lectures," in *Power/Knowledge*, 101–102.

17. *Discipline and Punish*, 137–38. Further, in the essay, "Nietzsche, Genealogy, History" (1971), which initiated his theoretical move to the sociohistorical (more accurately, what is for him the particularized "genealogical") analysis of power, Foucault, quoting Nietzsche, expressly links the pursuit of knowledge with bodily concerns. "Nietzsche, Genealogy, History," in *The Foucault Reader*, ed. Paul Rabinow (New York: Pantheon, 1984), 82–83.

18. "Two Lectures," in *Power/Knowledge*, 101.

19. *Discipline and Punish*, part 3, chap. 1.

20. Ibid., 141–69.

21. In his use of the word "disciplines," then, Foucault does not mean the human sciences themselves; he means disciplinary technologies, or practical mechanisms for establishing norms that produce and control the modern individual subject, which, "in the course of the seventeenth and eighteenth centuries became general formulas of domination." *Discipline and Punish*, 137.

22. "Two Lectures," in *Power/Knowledge*, 102.

23. Foucault, "Body/Power," in *Power/Knowledge*, 61.

24. Michel Foucault, *The Order of Things: An Archaeology of the Human Sciences*, trans. A. Sheridan (London: Tavistock, 1970), chap. 10. By "human science" Foucault means, at least roughly, what American intellectuals refer to as the social sciences and the humanities, and what German intellectuals mean by *Geisteswissenschaften*. Among the realms of knowledge that he regards as human sciences, Foucault explicitly includes psychology, sociology, the study of literature, cultural anthropology and ethnology,

psychiatry, and, to some degree, history.

25. "The Subject and Power," in *Beyond Structuralism and Hermeneutics*, 208.

26. Michel Foucault, *Madness and Civilization: A History of Insanity in the Age of Reason*, trans. R. Howard (New York: Random House, 1965); *The Birth of the Clinic: An Archaeology of Medical Perception*, trans. A. Sheridan (New York: Random House, 1975).

27. Michel Foucault, *The History of Sexuality. Volume 1: An Introduction*, trans. R. Hurley (New York: Random House, 1978); *Volume 2: The Use of Pleasure*, trans. R. Hurley (New York: Random House, 1985); *Volume 3: The Care of the Self*, trans. R. Hurley (New York: Random House, 1986).

28. *Discipline and Punish: The Birth of the Prison*, 296.

29. *Order of Things*, chap. 10.

30. Ibid., 344.

31. Ibid., 345–346.

32. Ibid., 363.

33. Ibid., 364.

34. Ibid., 363.

35. Ibid., 366–367.

36. *Beyond Structuralism and Hermeneutics*, 194.

37. Foucault defines *episteme* as "the total set of relations that unite, at a given period, the discursive practices that give rise to epistemological figures, sciences, and possibly formalized systems." *Archaeology of Knowledge*, trans. A. Sheridan (New York: Harper & Row, 1976), 191. *Dispositef* (translated as "apparatus"), which supplanted *episteme* in Foucault's later work, includes nondiscursive as well as discursive practices. "The Confession of the Flesh," in *Power/Knowledge*, 194–195. See also "The Subject and Power," in *Beyond Structuralism and Hermeneutics*, 208, 212.

38. *Discipline and Punish*, 305.

39. "The Subject and Power," in *Beyond Structuralism and Hermeneutics*, 212.

40. *Discipline and Punish*, 133.

41. Michel Foucault, "Intellectuals and Power," in *Language, Counter-Memory, Practice: Selected Essays and Interviews*, ed. Donald F. Bouchard (Ithaca: Cornell University Press, 1977), 207–208. See also "Truth and Power," in *Power/Knowledge*, 126–133.

42. *Discipline and Punish*, 133.

43. "Two Lectures," in *Power/Knowledge*, 95–98, 103–104; Michel Foucault, "Revolutionary Action: Until Now," in *Language, Counter-Memory, Practice:*, 221–222.

44. "The Subject and Power," in *Beyond Structuralism and Hermeneutics*, 212.

45. "Truth and Power," in *Power/Knowledge*, 118.

46. Michel Foucault, "Interview w/ Lucette Finas," in *Michel Foucault: Power, Truth, Strategy*, ed. M. Morris and P. Patton (Sydney: Feral, 1979), 75.

47. Jacques Derrida, *Of Grammatology*, trans. Gayatri Chakravorty Spivak (Baltimore: Johns Hopkins University Press, 1976), 3. Chakravorty Spivak's introduction is a widely regarded introduction to Derrida's thought. It provides illuminating comparisons and contrasts between Derrida and Nietzsche, Freud, Heidegger, and others. Other standard introductions that do the same are Christopher Norris, *Derrida* (Cambridge, Mass.: Harvard University Press, 1987); and Hilary Lawson, *Reflexivity:*

The Post-Modern Predicament (London: Hutchinson, 1985). Substantive philosophical critiques of Derrida are John Sallis, ed., *Deconstruction and Philosophy: The Texts of Jacques Derrida* (Chicago: University of Chicago Press, 1987); Rodolphe Gasche, *The Tain of the Mirror: Derrida and the Philosophy of Reflection* (Cambridge, Mass.: Harvard University Press, 1986); David Wood and Robert Bernasconi, eds., *Derrida and* Difference (Evanston: Northwestern University Press, 1988); and J. Claude Evans, *Strategies of Deconstruction: Derrida and the Myth of the Voice* (Minneapolis: University of Minnesota Press, 1991). The limited but growing attention paid to Derrida by Anglo-American philosophers is generally due to the "analytic" and "Continental" philosophical divide (see note 89 below). There are many other books on Derrida that approach him from a variety of perspectives; most often, he is analyzed by English and American scholars in terms of his implications for the study and critique of literature. One noteworthy example is Jonathan Culler's critically regarded *On Deconstruction: Theory and Criticism after Structuralism* (Ithaca: Cornell University Press, 1982), a particularly detailed exposition of Derrida's deconstructive strategies. Another is Eve Tavor Bannet, *Structuralism and the Logic of Dissent: Barthes, Derrida, Foucault, Lacan* (Urbana: University of Illinois Press, 1989). Tavor Bannet examines Derrida and some of the other notable French poststructuralists with particular attention for understanding them in terms of their distinctly French intellectual and sociocultural contexts. Her exposition suffers, however, from its attempt to import alienation, a modern notion, in order to illuminate poststructuralist thought. The idea of alienation presumes the possibility of individual autonomy, which, as I have made clear in my analysis of Foucault, is rejected by poststructuralists. Foucault, for example, would describe the concept of alienation, whether of the Marxist or existentialist variety, as a modern myth that perpetuates, rather than names, totalization.

Derrida is undoubtedly the most prolific French postmodern philosopher. Two collections of essays in which Derrida deconstructs important philosophical and literary texts are *Writing and Difference*, trans. Alan Bass (Chicago: University of Chicago Press, 1978), and *Margins of Philosophy*, trans. Alan Bass (Chicago: University of Chicago Press, 1982). These essays are diverse deconstructive exercises based on the ideas that Derrida developed in *Grammatology* and in *Speech and Phenomena and Other Essays on Husserl's Theory of Signs*, trans. David B. Allison (Evanston: Northwestern University Press, 1973). Extended deconstruction of philosophical texts is found in *Spurs: Nietzsche's Styles*, trans. Barbara Harlow (Chicago: University of Chicago Press, 1979); *Dissemination*, trans. Barbara Harlow (Chicago: University of Chicago Press, 1981); *Glas*, trans. John P. Leavey, Jr. and Richard Rand (Lincoln: University of Nebraska Press, 1986); *The Post Card: From Socrates to Freud and Beyond*, trans. Alan Bass (Chicago: University of Chicago Press, 1987); *The Archeology of the Frivolous: Reading Condillac*, trans. John P. Leavey (Lincoln: University of Nebraska Press, 1987); *The Truth in Painting*, trans. Geoffrey Bennington and Ian McLeod (Chicago: University of Chicago Press, 1987); and *Of Spirit: Heidegger and the Question*, trans. Geoffrey Bennington and Rachel Bowlby (Chicago: University of Chicago Press, 1989). Most of these works use deconstructive strategies that emphasize a variety of unconventional literary nuances to deconstruct philosophical oppositions. Of course, Derrida rejects a stable distinction between philosophy and literature. Every act of general writing that Derrida engages in reflects, among other things, his incessant deconstruction of that distinction: the philosopher and the writer are the same, but not identical. It is common for Derrida to juxtapose philosophical and literary texts with his "own" in order to deconstruct this very distinction; the most explicit example of this strategy is *Glas*. Derrida has written two rather unilluminating essays on higher education that have been translated into English. "The Principle of Reason: The University in the Eyes of its Pupils," *Diacritics* 13 (Fall, 1983): 3–20, discusses the social responsibility of universities. "Mochlos; or, The Conflict of the Faculties," in Richard Rand, ed., *Logomachia: The Conflict of the Faculties* (Lincoln: University of Nebraska, 1992), 3–34, explores this theme further, by analyzing the thought of Kant on the idea of a university. In "Canons and Metonymies: An Interview with Jacques Derrida," Derrida discusses this topic and others further on pages 195–218.

48. In Heidegger's terms, for example, this notion would be the "Being of beings." Martin Heidegger, *Basic Writings*, ed. David Farrell Krell (New York: Harper & Row, 1977). Derrida's early works articulate his basic argument; his later works are attempts to apply his argument by deconstruction of various foundational texts. This argument is found in its most extensive and detailed exposition in *Grammatology*.

49. Jacques Derrida, "Semiology and Grammatology," in *Positions*, trans. Alan Bass, (Chicago: University of Chicago, 1981), 19.

50. *Grammatology*, 14–15.

51. Ibid., 10–18.

52. Ibid., 18.

53. Ibid., 15.

54. Ibid., 29–41.

55. Ibid., 43.

56. Ibid., 16–17.

57. Ibid., 73.

58. Jacques Derrida, "Differance," in *Speech and Phenomena*, 139–141. Another translation of this essay can be found in *Margins of Philosophy*, trans. Alan Bass (Chicago: University of Chicago Press, 1982), 1–27.

59. Ibid., 133, 139–140.

60. *Grammatology*, 34.

61. Ibid., 45–46.

62. Ibid., 38, 30–41; "Semiology and Grammatology," in *Positions*, 21–25.

63. *Grammatology*, 30.

64. Ibid., 44–45.

65. Ibid.

66. Ibid., 46.

67. "Differance," in *Speech and Phenomena*, 133.

68. Ibid., 133–34.

69. Ibid., 132.

70. Ibid., 129. Derrida is careful not to make truth claims about differance: differance is itself subject to deconstruction, it is never pure. *Grammatology*, 143. Differance is then the same, but not identical with, other Derridian deconstructive terms like *trace, supplement,* and *gramme*.

71. "Differance," in *Speech and Phenomena*, 136–152.

72. Ibid., 129.

73. Ibid.

74. "Semiology and Grammatology," in *Positions*, 19.

75. "Differance," 135.
76. Derrida, "Positions," in *Positions*, 42–43.
77. *Grammatology*, 38–39.
78. Ibid., 36.
79. "Arche" signifies that general writing is the writing of differance: it indicates that for Derrida knowledge of the pervasiveness of writing in general is not an absolute, because it too is subject to differance. *Grammatology*, 56–57, 61–62. See also Derrida, "The Original Discussion of *Différance* (1968)," in *Derrida and* Difference, 84–85.
80. "Semiology and Grammatology," in *Positions*, 44–45.
81. *Grammatology*, 9.
82. Derrida, "Implications," in *Positions*, 14.
83. *Grammatology*, 66.
84. "Semiology and Grammatology," in *Positions*, 26–27.
85. Ibid., 27.
86. "Differance," in *Speech and Phenomena*, 154.
87. *Grammatology*, 86.
88. "Positions," in *Positions*, 49.
89. "Positions," in *Positions*, 52.
90. Searle attacks Derrida and those who have been influenced by deconstruction on the basis of "the low level of philosophical argumentation, the deliberate obscuratism of the prose, the wildly exaggerated claims, and the constant striving to give the appearance of profundity by making claims that seem paradoxical, but under analysis often turn out to be silly or trivial." John Searle, "Reply to Louis H. Mackay," *New York Review of Books* 31, no. 1 (1984): 48. Searle thus continues a tradition among some Anglo-American philosophers to simply refuse to consider Continental philosophers on their own terms, perhaps inaugurated by Rudolf Carnap's ridicule of Heidegger (cited in Arthur C. Danto, *Connections to the World* (New York: Harper & Row, 1989), 60–62. See also Searle's "Reiterating the Differences: A Reply to Derrida," *Glyph* 1 (1977): 198–208; "The World Turned Upside Down," *New York Review of Books*, 30, no. 16 (1983): 74–79; and *Intentionality: An Essay in the Philosophy of Mind* (Cambridge, U. K.: Cambridge University Press, 1983). Jonathan Culler calls Searle's position on Derrida an "egregious misunderstanding" in his book *On Deconstruction: Theory and Criticism After Structuralism* (Ithaca, N. Y.: Cornell University Press, 1982), 112. For Derrida's reply to Searle, see Jacques Derrida, *Limited, Inc.* (Baltimore: Johns Hopkins Press, 1988). For similar criticism of Derrida, see J. Claude Evans, *Strategies of Deconstruction: Derrida and the Myth of the Voice* (Minneapolis: University of Minnesota Press, 1991); Hilary Putnam, *Renewing Philosophy* (Cambridge, Mass.: Harvard University Press, 1992), 126–33; John Passmore, *Recent Philosophers* (La Salle, Ill.: Open Court, 1990), 27–33.
91. "Semiology and Grammatology," in *Positions*, 17. See also Jacques Derrida, "Structure, Sign, and Play in the Discourse of the Human Sciences," in *Writing and Difference*, 280; Jacques Derrida, "The Supplement of Copula: Philosophy Before Linguistics," in *Margins of Philosophy*, 177.
92. "Positions," in *Positions*, 59.
93. *Grammatology*, 9.

Past, Present, and Possibility

> In order to do interdisciplinary work, it is not enough to take a "subject" (a theme) and to arrange two or three sciences around it. Interdisciplinary study consists in creating a new object.[1]

The aim of this chapter is to begin to develop the basis for an alternative idea of inquiry that follows from my analysis of postmodern critiques. This analysis has led to the idea that contemporary inquiry is subject to a basic condition that arises from a relationship with the past. Further, postmodern critique suggests that this relationship is an unnecessary and undesirable constraint or impediment on the range of activities in which scholars may engage in an inquiry. The questions that I will pursue in this chapter are: (1) What is the basic condition of modern inquiry in relation to the past? (2) How does it act as a constraint on intellect? and (3) Why is this constraint undesirable?

THE BASIC CONDITION OF INQUIRY IN RELATION TO THE PAST

What is the basic condition of inquiry in relation to the past? It is the belief that the essential foundation of inquiry in the university is pursuit of knowledge of phenomena that are assumed to (1) exist before and independent of inquiry, and (2) persist essentially unchanged by inquiry. For the sake of convenience, I will simply use the phrase "preexistent reality" to signify (1) and (2). Embedded in this often tacit belief is an assumption concerning the idea of knowledge at its most fundamental level, which involves a certain characterization of a relationship between intellect and reality. Intellect is a thing that seeks to explain the behavior of things and problems that are "already there," whether they are thought to preexist with or without human involvement.

Within this concept, scientific study of things that are thought to exist independent of human involvement, namely the natural and physical sciences and mathematics, are often accorded preeminence in the university relative to the social sciences and the humanities, on the basis that the former produces objective, "real" knowledge, or far more nearly so. Indeed, some scholars believe that the value of the social sciences and even the humanities is a function of the extent that scholars in these fields are able to construct and utilize methods that are modeled on those of the natural and physical sciences and mathematics so as to produce "real" knowledge.

Based on this characterization of intellect and reality, inquiry stresses the role of theory. Theory is the bridge between intellect and preexistent reality. For this reason, theoretical knowledge of reality is the most fundamental knowledge. Since theory is about some aspect of reality that is thought to be essentially autonomous of inquiry, a good theory is, among other things, not essentially a human creation. Instead, it is a human re-creation of reality in the form of an explanation of the way something is independent of the knower. A good theory is transparent; it "mirrors" reality. In doing so, it signifies in words that the theorist comprehends the kinds of things that the theory explains. In the modern university the status of theory gives it a quality that approaches the autonomy of its object.

Similarly, the practice of pursuing theoretical knowledge of preexistent reality is given a special status relative to other practices in higher education. Theoretical knowledge is the foundation for practical knowledge, and theoretical activity is the foundation of practical activity. Typically, these distinctions are sharply drawn within modern research and comprehensive universities. The kinds of inquiries and other intellectual activities that occur in professional, applied, and artistic schools and departments are usually considered separate from inquiries of schools and departments that pursue basic research. While the first kind of activities may be very strong in particular schools, the second kind are generally regarded to be the core of a university and, therefore, the most significant barometer of its overall strength and reputation. Further, the strongest professional, applied, and art schools are usually considered to be those where the value of theory for practice is stressed. Other intellectual and practical activities are deemed intellectually inferior to the pursuit of theoretical knowledge, because they are tarnished by the lack of autonomous objects. Typically, they borrow knowledge from, or gain knowledge from applying, the results obtained in the pursuit of theoretical knowledge.

Most importantly, these other intellectual and practical activities must themselves borrow the idea of theory from basic science and gain theoretical knowledge of practice. Even theoretical knowledge of practice is considered to be inferior to theoretical knowledge of reality independent of practice because it is at a second remove from the essence of theory, namely, theory that explains aspects of autonomous reality. Therefore, the pursuit of theoretical knowledge of reality is considered a special case of practice. It is the practice of gaining access, however partial and imperfect, to things that are independent of the knower and thus independent of the practice that accesses it.

One objection to the claim that inquiry is essentially about knowledge of a preexistent reality is that other basic purposes of higher education are equally or more important, such as the transmission of knowledge, the education of enlightened citizens, the application of knowledge to practical problems, and the training of professionals.[2] However, it is generally held or implied that fulfillment of these other purposes is dependent on there being knowledge of preexistent reality to transmit and apply. For this reason, the pursuit of knowledge of preexistent reality is, in practice, considered to be foundational in its function. This is at least one important reason why research universities are regarded as being of the highest stature. Institutions of higher learning where research is not emphasized nevertheless seek teachers who have been educated in research universities, who have engaged in scholarly research, and who have doctoral degrees reflecting knowledge of research methods and research skills.

A second objection is that even if the pursuit of knowledge of preexistent reality is a basic condition of contemporary inquiry, it could still be considered to serve purely or primarily instrumental reasons relative to the other purposes that I have mentioned. The position that the value of higher education is primarily instrumental has a long tradition, especially as a common belief held among many people outside the university. This position is reflected, for example, in the emergence of comprehensive universities over the last one hundred years, in the widespread attitude in society that a college education, including the liberal arts, is necessary preparation for a professional career, and in the intense competition for public and corporate funds devoted to applied research. Each of these factors, along with numerous others, suggests that many people consider the university to be a place for ends that are not strictly determined by the pursuit of knowledge. Further, many people hold that the extent that higher education satisfies these ends determines the value of that pursuit.

However, most within the modern university do not think of their work as primarily instrumental in nature. They at least tacitly believe that the foundation provided by the pursuit of preexistent reality is independent of instrumental purposes. This independence is associated with belief in an idea of reality as essentially preexistent, and of knowledge of preexistent reality as being intrinsically valuable independent of any other purpose than its own. Indeed, it is arguable that an implicit justification for academic freedom is grounded in the belief that inquiry pursues knowledge of objects that are independent and objective, rather than being only arbitrary, even if the pursuit of knowledge for its own sake is descriptive of inquiry generally.

COLLECTIVE PROGRESS

The cognitive, sensory, and physical limitations of theoretical knowledge are mediated by the idea that particular understandings gained in the pursuit of knowledge are contributions toward a comprehensive, increasingly accurate understanding of reality. Also, the limitations of theory are mediated by a collective ideal, which is manifested in a conception of the university as, or as growing into being, a coherent, unified whole. Theories are the basis of this ideal conception, which considers theories collectively to comprise an integrated, comprehensive hierarchy or order of explanations of reality that form a coherent whole. Theoretical knowledge is seen to accumulate progressively, serving the aim either of "filling in," and/or of gradually reconstructing more effectively a complete or whole picture called reality. In this way, a particular theory takes on meaning that extends beyond the meaning that it has as one theory alone. Knowledge of reality has a collective meaning as an integrated collection of particular theoretical representations of particular aspects of a single, unified reality. Knowledge of the whole is a collective endeavor of inquirers over time, who, as individual participants of an intellectual community, seek to contribute toward the incremental accumulation of particular theories that are to make up knowledge of this whole. This overall conception is variously expressed by each of the modern thinkers that I examined in Chapter 2.

Although many intellectuals today deny the claim that there really is a whole picture that is completely or essentially knowable, or knowable with absolute certainty, it is still common to think that theoretical knowledge progresses toward at least an approximation of such ideals. The idea of a progression here suggests a linear movement toward something that is stable and independent of that movement, something that is the telos of the movement. Even if belief in "complete" or "perfect" knowledge of reality is explicitly rejected, this idea of a progression of theoretical knowledge is, as an underlying aim, implicit in the claim that explanations of reality are improved upon or are succeeded by better explanations.

Moreover, denial of the notion that the collective pursuit of "complete knowledge" is what unifies the modern university, even if that notion is not actually believed or even considered by a great many among its faculties, without offering well-formed proposals for an alternative conception, only shows that philosophically the modern idea of higher education as a communal endeavor remains tacitly dependent on it. If, or to the extent that, this idea is no longer believed, the question arises as to how any particular pursuit of theoretical knowledge can be thought to refer to anything besides itself. Clearly, few modern scholars would find this description of their work desirable.

THE PREEXISTENT REALITY OF THE DISCIPLINES

Most scholars today would say that their inquiries seek to discover, improve, and enlarge knowledge within their particular disciplines. In the modern university, the pursuit of preexistent reality primarily takes place in disciplines, which are forms or categories of knowledge of preexistent reality. In effect, the disciplines are the manifestation of the basic condition of inquiry, and for several reasons. First, the disciplines that are composed of the natural sciences, the social sciences, and the humanities are generally regarded as comprising the foundations of the university in practice. Second, the disciplines, as currently practiced, are primarily concerned with theoretical knowledge of reality as I have described it, namely, as knowledge of preexistent reality. Third, in large part, since theory is expressed in disciplinary terms, the disciplines are the prescribed structure for intellectual activity.

For these reasons, the basic disciplines are, in effect, generally regarded as if they are a basic condition of inquiry and the essential foundation for what counts as legitimate intellectual activity in universities and colleges. Further, in this organized pursuit of knowledge, "preexistent reality" is, in effect, the disciplinary structure of inquiry. This effect occurs in terms of both theory (of knowledge) and practice (institutional organization of inquiry and curricula, individual career paths and peer affiliations, and reward systems).

One objection to this claim is that it does not take account of the nature of inquiry within applied and professional fields, and the pervasiveness of these fields in higher education institutions. Even if they borrow theory heavily from the disciplines, applied and professional fields are not essentially about explaining preexistent reality. Rather, they are concerned with explaining practical conditions and concepts, and most significantly, with devising solutions and innovations. Therefore, even if they do not have the stature within higher education of the disciplines, the different nature of their inquiry, coupled with their significant presence in higher education institutions, refutes the claim that inquiry is essentially about explaining preexistent reality.

There are several responses to this position. First, the problems of applied and professional fields are problems that are assumed to exist before and independent of inquiry. Second, even if inquiry in these fields places an emphasis on devising solutions to practical problems, rather than explaining preexistent reality, these solutions are responses to problems that are assumed to exist before and independent of inquiry, and to that significant extent, are determined by that basic condition. Third, like the disciplines that influence them, the theories of applied and professional fields have an autonomy apart from inquiry such that they have the same effect on inquiry as the disciplines. Like the disciplines, they are "subjects" of inquiry that are assumed to have an essentially stable and permanent existence. Like the disciplines, they are, in effect, the preexistent reality of inquiry, though they do not have the stature of the disciplines.

A second objection to the claim that the basic condition of inquiry is the disciplinary pursuit of knowledge of preexistent reality is the presence and growth of interdisciplinary inquiry. Interdisciplinarity is a commonly discussed alternative to the disciplinary pursuit of knowledge.[3] It is often presented in the context of a critique of the disciplines. However, interdisciplinary inquiry emerges in response to problems defined in terms of the disciplines, and it is usually advanced as a way of enhancing the disciplinary pursuit of knowledge of reality.

Most significantly, the emphasis of interdisciplinarity is on the unification of knowledge as a whole. Like the disciplines, interdisciplinarity is implicitly an idea of a unified, whole reality. It does not replace the disciplines but fills in alleged gaps between them by creating "cross-disciplines" that are in effect additional disciplines. The purpose of going "between" the disciplines is to realize a broader, more complete, and integrated understanding of phenomena than is afforded by any single discipline. Modern interdisciplinarity seeks to resolve sharp disciplinary distinctions in order to render the pursuit of knowledge into a coherent totality. It tries to repair the modern fragmentation of knowledge and bring the disciplines together so that the disciplinary project of knowledge of reality can be realized. For these reasons, interdisciplinarity is largely an uncritical extension of the disciplines rather than a critical alternative. Interdisciplinarity functions, in practice as opposed to rhetoric, as a logical implication of the disciplines and defines itself in terms of them.

A third objection is that at least for some lines of inquiry within some disciplines, the pursuit of knowledge is intended to gain knowledge of preexisting reality in order to change it. These lines of inquiry can be found especially in sociology, anthropology, history, and political science, and in applied fields as well. However, a distinction between pursuit of knowledge and critique is common, in which the latter is largely viewed as being less important than the former by scholars. Further, inquiry that is motivated by a desire to change the social or political order of a society, for example, usually does not actually pursue change in the course of inquiry, with the exception of so-called "action research."[4]

THE DISCIPLINES AND PROGRESS

The ancient idea that knowledge of reality can be classified into a hierarchy of discrete categories was initially developed in greatest depth by Aristotle. These classifications included, first, the theoretical sciences, which seek knowledge for its own sake, and include the disciplines of metaphysics, physics, and mathematics; second, the practical sciences, which aim for knowledge as a guide to good conduct; and third, productive sciences, which are comprised of knowledge for making useful or beautiful things.[5] In the schools of ancient Greece, seven basic disciplines were distinguished and placed in two groups, known later in Roman civilization as the *trivium* and the *quadrivium*. The *trivium* consisted of grammar, logic, and rhetoric; the *quadrivium* was composed of arithmetic, geometry, astronomy, and musical theory. With occasional variation, these seven *disciplinae liberales* or *artes liberales* were subsequently adapted as the basic curriculum in the Christian universities of the Middle Ages and were preparatory for advanced education in theology, law, and medicine.[6] Although the medieval curriculum has not survived as the core of the modern university, the idea that knowledge of reality conforms to categories or disciplines remains the essential logic on which the modern pursuit of knowledge is organized. In the modern university, the disciplines are basic structures of knowledge that in effect shape a priori just what reality shall mean in terms of the content and pursuit of knowledge.

The idea that there are discrete categories of knowledge of reality is usually taken to imply that although the theories found within a category are diverse, and often embody alternative accounts, they nevertheless share some fundamental, meaningful inherent characteristics. That is, the fact that there are categories of knowledge reflects the belief that particular pieces of knowledge share common features that justifies grouping them together in a category. These common features have to do with the subject matter of a discipline. The subject matter indicates how reality is conceived and what aspects of reality are studied in a discipline. In this limited but significant sense, the knowledge within each discipline or category is unified and forms a unique self-encompassing whole. In a broader sense, this idea of a unified disciplinary whole is that, ideally, particular inquiries within a discipline are contributions toward the progressive realization of a coherent body of knowledge. In both of these senses, the idea of disciplinary knowledge suggests that reality and knowledge of reality are stable and orderly.

Another basic attribute of categories or disciplines of knowledge, in the modern university at least, is that theoretical knowledge progresses dynamically within the disciplines. This dynamism is reflected in the increasing depth and diversity of theoretical explanations, methods, and schools of thought that emerge over time. It can be conceptualized in terms of depth and breadth. First, the pursuit of knowledge within the disciplines is dynamic in depth in the sense that existing theories are developed, refined, and extended. Further, existing theories are replaced by new theories that are deemed to be better explanations. Second, intellectual activity within the disciplines is dynamic in breadth. That is, new modes of inquiry, or subdisciplines, creating new kinds of theoretical knowledge, emerge within the disciplines alongside established modes. Sometimes a new mode of inquiry replaces an established mode, but more often the former are additions to the latter, and the theoretical knowledge they provide takes a place next to the theoretical knowledge that is already in the discipline. Although there are disputes about what constitutes legitimate modes of inquiry, subject matter, and theories with a given discipline, the disputes are usually incorporated into the discipline along with the new ideas. Indeed, the presence of theoretical, methodological, and philosophical disputes is usually interpreted to mean that a discipline is in a "healthy" state.

Thus, if one looks within the disciplines, at the theories, methods, and "schools of thought" that they contain, the disciplines are dynamic. It would seem, then, that rejection of the foundational stature of the disciplines is patently undesirable because the pursuit of knowledge in the order of these structures is very productive. However, an important distinction can be made between the disciplines as structures that contain knowledge, on one hand, and the contents of these structures, on the other hand. In other words, one cannot simply assume that the disciplines and their contents are identical. I stated above that the dynamism of the disciplines is a characteristic of their contents. What effects does the dynamism of the pursuit of knowledge within the disciplines have on the disciplines as structures of knowledge? The increasing depth and diversity of theoretical knowledge within the disciplines means that the disciplines are expanding, in that they encompass ever-increasing quantities of knowledge. Indeed, the idea that modern inquiry is progressive over time is most visible in this sense.

THE CONSTRAINT OF THE DISCIPLINES ON INTELLECT

The expansion of disciplinary knowledge can be interpreted as a sign that the disciplines are robust structures. However, it can also be interpreted to mean that the disciplines are increasingly incoherent structures. That is, the dynamic production of knowledge within the disciplines renders the disciplines as structures of knowledge increasingly unintelligible. In this regard, expansion in breadth is particularly significant. The profusion of new, diverse modes of inquiry, especially in the last thirty years, has destabilized the disciplines. The increasing diversity of modes of inquiry has made it difficult to view disciplines as coherent knowledge realms.

The most significant evidence of this incoherence is the "blurring" of disciplinary boundaries as a result of intellectual activity that pursues knowledge by combining, or seeking to combine, theories or modes of inquiry from more than one discipline. The diverse expansion of inquiry is partly an overlapping of disciplinary boundaries. It is often not clear under which discipline a cross-disciplinary mode of inquiry properly belongs. Unity and autonomy would seem to be presupposed by the fact that the disciplines structure the pursuit of knowledge a priori as discrete realms. Yet the increasing diversity of inquiry, especially the blurring of disciplinary boundaries, suggests that the disciplines are fragmented rather than unified, autonomous wholes. If so, then the order that they impose a priori for the pursuit of knowledge is not a posteriori justified.

It could be argued that interdisciplinary institutes, if well conceived, may adequately cure disciplinary fragmentation. However, although the emergence of interdisciplinary institutes such as regional studies may mediate fragmentation to some extent, institutes do not make the disciplines more coherent. In fact, their emergence can be interpreted as an indication of fragmentation. Moreover, interdisciplinary institutes, which are in a stage of infancy, are themselves not particularly coherent. In addition, they are often considered less important than the disciplines. At least in part, they can be viewed as modest stopgap efforts to accommodate the fragmentation of the disciplines. Thus, interdisciplinary institutes solidify the absolute effect of the disciplines despite disciplinary fragmentation. Institutes do not, however, cure the incoherence of the disciplines. Nor do they really challenge the viability of the disciplines. They are sites where modes of inquiry across disciplines can be combined outside the disciplines that has the effect of preserving the absoluteness of the disciplines.

Yet even if the disciplines are fragmented structures, this condition can itself be interpreted to mean that the disciplinary pursuit of knowledge is a productive and creative foundation for intellectual activity. That is, it could be claimed that the disciplines have proven to be flexible structures in that they expand to accommodate new approaches and ideas that emerge within them. In addition, new disciplines emerge on occasion when new realms of knowledge of reality are discovered. On this basis, it could be argued that the absolute status of the disciplines is justified even if they are fragmented. Further, even if fragmentation means that the disciplines are not unified wholes, it could be argued that the grouping of knowledge according to disciplinary structures is justified on the basis that these structures are effective in maximizing the production of knowledge. It might even be argued that having categories of knowledge is justified simply because they provide a convenient way of managing the rapid production and enormous amount of diverse knowledge. For these reasons, the essentialist stature of the disciplines could be defended even though they are increasingly fragmented.

How, then, is the foundational status of the disciplines an unjustified constraint on inquiry? Depth and breadth are only two dimensions. If this metaphor is a reasonable portrayal of the disciplinary pursuit of knowledge, it suggests that knowledge can only be conceptualized, and progress, in a field or plane constituted by "flat," all-encompassing disciplinary structures, just as a round marble cannot leave the floor on which it rolls and still be a marble except in name only. The seemingly limitless potentiality of reality and knowledge is severely limited by the assumption that a person who is seriously engaged in an intellectual activity for the purpose of enlarging human understanding cannot leave this plane. One can only enlarge or diminish it.

Further, although the pursuit of knowledge within the disciplines is dynamic, the reality that is already there, in the form of theories, methods, and schools of thought, largely determines what reality can mean for inquiry. The progress of knowledge usually proceeds along paths that have been determined in the past. Even if disciplinary boundaries are blurred the disciplinary plane remains, just as the paper on which two colors of paint are mixed remains. Therefore, even if the disciplines are flexible to a degree, they are not so flexible as their foundational stature would seem to require, assuming that the core value of academic freedom implies in part that the pursuit of knowledge is potentially limitless.

Yet, it can be argued that the disciplinary pursuit of knowledge can be construed as providing potentially limitless possibilities for knowledge. The ideal of free inquiry has meaning and value partly on the assumption that there are no bounds to what the pursuit of knowledge of reality may reveal. Therefore, the pursuit of knowledge should not be constrained by any principles that might impede the capacity of intellect to inquire, apart from ethical considerations concerning the means of the pursuit. However, the pursuit of preexistent reality is itself a constraining principle. It is only *within* this principle that the possibilities of thought are allowed to be potentially limitless.

Rejection of the foundational stature of the disciplinary pursuit of knowledge of reality is desirable, then, because it would expand the possibilities for fruitful intellectual activity by making it easier to move inquiry off of the "disciplinary plane." The dynamism of what occurs within the disciplines is an indication that the disciplines as they are constituted are fertile grounds for the growth of knowledge to some extent. However, this dynamism can be interpreted, at least in part, to mean that thought strives to go beyond the disciplines. Similarly, the blurring of disciplinary boundaries is only a relatively small indication of where progressive inquiry can go, since this blurring is largely, or perhaps even exclusively, confined to the disciplinary plane and, therefore, does not significantly challenge the foundational stature of the disciplines and the kind of pursuit of knowledge that they manifest. This does not mean that the pursuit of knowledge of reality would or the disciplines would disappear. It does mean, however, that the disciplines would be resituated so that they would not largely determine the shape of legitimate intellectual activity.

THE PROBLEM: RESITUATION OF THE DISCIPLINES

The problem, then, is how to construe and resituate the disciplines in a way that removes their effect as unnecessarily constraining foundational structures, while retaining the vitality of inquiry within them, so that the pursuit of knowledge is expanded, and the range of possibilities for what constitutes legitimate intellectual activity is broadened. If the guide to this resituation is nascent in the disciplines, what is this guide? Since the blurring of disciplinary boundaries is a significant challenge to the stature of the disciplines, because it creates the ground for new opportunities by destabilizing those boundaries, it would seem that resituation of the disciplines would extend this idea in some way. The blurring of boundaries suggests that even though the disciplines as structures are foundational, some intellectual activity within the disciplines does not follow this principle but is trying in part to move out of these boundaries. Cross-disciplinary inquiries are efforts to pursue knowledge without being essentially constrained by the structure and content of a single discipline, including subject matter, predominant theories, typical methods, or primary schools of thought.

Thus, cross-disciplinary efforts imply a general desire to conceive knowledge and inquiry in new ways. This general desire can be understood as two basic themes underlying cross-disciplinarity that together can be used as a guide for an idea of inquiry that does not give the disciplines the stature of an essential foundation. First, cross-disciplinarity suggests an emphasis on the particularity of inquiry. Since cross-disciplinarity involves a transgression of the disciplines as singular, bounded wholes, it violates the mandate that inquiry be essentially grounded in knowledge structures that are already there, before inquiry. Cross-disciplinary inquiry can be interpreted as manifesting a desire to allow the impetus of a particular inquiry to not be bound or constrained by established theoretical parameters, metaframeworks, and modes of inquiry. For this reason, cross-disciplinarity suggests an idea of inquiry in which an inquirer essentially constructs a particular ground in the course of inquiry in ways that do not require adherence to a prevailing disciplinary or an interdisciplinary approach. One might think of this process as something like composing a narrative, in that the ground of a particular inquiry is shaped by what emerges in the course of that inquiry itself.

LEAVING THE DISCIPLINARY PLANE

The second theme underlying cross-disciplinarity that can be used as a basis for an alternative idea of inquiry is a general desire to not be constrained by what I have called the disciplinary plane and by the idea that inquiry is essentially pursuit of preexistent reality. Cross-disciplinary inquiries manifest not only the desire to traverse the boundaries of specific disciplines; they also display a general desire to traverse this boundary, preexistent reality, and the disciplines as this boundary's collective manifestation.

This means that theoretical knowledge would not be limited to explanations of what is already there or elaborations of such explanations. In addition, theoretical knowledge would include particular expressions, proposals, and visions of how reality can be conceived and what it can become. Further, if knowledge is produced in the course of particular inquiries, then these inquiries could move off or leave the disciplinary plane. Leaving this plane would mean leaving the idea that one studies what is already there.

This implication suggests that resituating the disciplines would mean creating a space outside the disciplines and interdisciplines. The blurring of the pursuit of knowledge and its object involves conceiving a space that is outside disciplinary boundaries as well as conceiving relationships between this space and disciplinary inquiries. Further, the idea that the disciplines function as a foundational boundary suggests a boundary that is self-enclosed. A boundary creates two spaces, a space inside and a space outside the boundary, and these two sides are kept from each other by virtue of the boundary. Therefore, rejection of the foundational stature of the disciplines also implies opening up a relationship between a space outside the boundaries and the space within them.

BEGINNINGS OF NEW GROUNDS FOR INQUIRY

The two themes that I have derived and amplified from cross-disciplinarity suggest that rejection of the pursuit of knowledge of reality and of its collective manifestation in the form of disciplinary foundations provides a beginning for grounds that make plausible new forms of knowledge. Rejection of this foundation in the practice of higher education would mean an expansion of the possibilities for fruitful intellectual activity by making it possible to move inquiry off of the disciplinary plane and thereby create new planes or foundations. In these ways, postmodern inquiry would open up the complex, interactive, varied relationship between knowers and reality, and would, therefore, liberate intellectual community and legitimate intellectual activity from the constraining effect of the disciplinary knowledge of reality. It would create and institute a legitimate space for post-objectivisitic and post-subjectivistic ideas concerning reality, knower, and knowledge of reality.

However, assuming that the idea of preexistent reality, an idea that has served as the productive foundation of Western inquiry for 2600 years, cannot be simply transcended, this conception must retain this idea. The problem that this chapter leaves for further development, then, is that an alternative idea of inquiry must be based on a philosophical foundation that passes beyond the disciplinary pursuit of preexistent reality, yet is capable of sustaining the latter in a form that does not preclude or constrain other potential forms of inquiry.

In Chapter 6, I propose a philosophical foundation for inquiry that builds on the implications that I derived from the five postmodern critiques and that creates a space for particular inquiries that are not about knowing preexisting reality and that, therefore, do not conform with disciplinary norms. It is a foundation that makes room for intellectual activity outside the sorts of relationship between knower and reality normally assumed in the original project of modernity defined most prominently in the French Enlightenment and by modern successors such as the various brands of positivistic thought. What is needed to make this possible is a broader notion of inquiry than the pursuit of knowledge of preexistent reality. This broader notion will imply that there can be other ideas of knowledge and inquiry that are justified in themselves in some contingent sense, but no more than the pursuit of knowledge is contingent on the idea that a theory must refer to preexistent reality. The foundation that is aimed for is one that will be useful rather than essential. By this statement, I mean that the foundation to be produced will be one whose essential purpose is to make lots of intellectual room for intellect to pursue inquiries that are not grounded in the idea of a preexistent reality, including room for the basic idea that inquiry need not follow existing ideas of what it means to engage in an inquiry.

NOTES

1. Barthes, Roland. "Research: The Young," In *The Rustle of Language* (New York: Hill and Wang, 1986), 72.

2. An objection to the claim that the pursuit of preexisting reality has historically been the primary paradigm for the liberal arts curriculum in the modern period is that rhetorical forms of education have long held a significant place in institutions of higher education. See Bruce A. Kimball, *Orators and Philosophers: A History of the Idea of Liberal Education* (New York: Teachers College Press, 1986). However, Kimball acknowledges that the pursuit of knowledge has generally dominated the liberal arts curriculum, especially since the rise of modern research universities in the nineteenth and twentieth centuries. Further, while largely nonphilosophical forms of rhetoric derived from classical and medieval thought have dominated modern conceptions of education, these conceptions presuppose, as the eighteenth-century French encyclopedists did, a grammar that builds from letters to phrases and sentences to larger forms of descriptive, explanatory, and persuasive discourse, and that gets translated into conceptions of a rationally and/or empirically apprehended universe. Thus, the rather sharply drawn historical distinction between philosophical and rhetorical forms that Kimball makes, and upon which his thesis relies, is questionable. For some initial indications of a marked contrast between historical developments in philosophy and those in rhetoric, see Terrence N. Tice and Thomas P. Slavens, *Research Guide to Philosophy* (Chicago: American Library Association, 1983).

3. See for instance Julie Thompson Klein, *Interdisciplinarity: History, Theory, and Practice* (Detroit: Wayne University Press, 1990); Mary E. Clark and Sandra A. Wawrytko, eds., *Rethinking the Curriculum: Toward an Integrated, Interdisciplinary College Education* (Westport, Conn.: Greenwood Press, 1990); Joseph J. Kockelmans, ed., *Interdisciplinarity and Higher Education* (University Park: Pennsylvania State University Press, 1979). For a modern critique of the first two books, see Roger P. Mourad, Jr., "The Case for Interdisciplinary Knowledge and Practice: A Review of *Interdisciplinarity* and *Rethinking the Curriculum*," *The Review of Higher Education* 16, no. 2 (Winter 1993): 127–140.

4. Foucault speaks to this condition critically when he asserts that the aim for intellectuals should not be to stand off to the side of others in order to express the "stifled truth of the collectivity," but rather, should be to struggle against forms of power that transform them into its object and instrument. Michel Foucault, "Intellectuals and Power," in *Language, Counter-Memory, Practice: Selected Essays and Interviews*, ed. Donald F. Bouchard (Ithaca: Cornell University Press, 1977), 207–208. See also Michel Foucault, "Truth and Power," in *Power/Knowledge: Selected Interviews and Other Writings*, ed. Colin Gordon (New York: Random House, 1980), 126–133.

5. Aristotle, *Metaphysics*, trans. W. Jaeger (Oxford: Oxford Classical Texts, 1957), Book VI, 1025b.

6. Kimball, *Orators and Philosophers*, chap. 2; John W. Baldwin, *The Scholastic Culture of the Middle Ages, 1000–1300* (Lexington, Mass.: D. C. Heath, 1971), 62–67.

6

Expanded Grounds for Inquiry:
The Pursuit of Intellectually Compelling Ideas

> The work of philosophical and historical reflection is put back into the field of the work of thought only on condition that one clearly grasps problemization not as an arrangement of representations but as a work of thought.[1]

In the preceding chapter, I claimed that modern inquiry is conditioned upon a relation with the past that serves as its ground, that this condition is that inquiry is essentially the pursuit of preexistent reality, and that the disciplines manifest this condition preeminently, although applied and professional fields are also implicated. In order to make it possible for other forms of inquiry to be created and develop, it is necessary to develop a foundation for inquiry that includes, but is not constrained by, the idea of preexistent reality. In this chapter, I will pursue this task. This alternative foundation will answer the question of what it means to expand what counts for legitimate intellectual activity. Since I have emphasized that this foundation would liberate individual inquiries from having to be bound by preexisting reality, my starting point is to analyze fundamentally the idea of an individual inquiry in detail.

INQUIRY AS A DETERMINATION OF REALITY

The development of an alternative foundation requires that the core of the idea of preexistent reality be resituated in a way that does not limit inquiry to the pursuit of preexistent reality a priori. This core is located in the relationship between the basic constituents of modern inquiry, namely, inquirer, reality, and knowledge. The ensuing analysis is not intended to be the "right" analysis of this relationship, in the sense of explaining the way this relationship "really is." Rather, it is meant to be a useful one for the purpose that I have specified.

Further, although I will emphasize resituating disciplines, I also mean to include applied, professional, and interdisciplinary fields on the basis that they also adhere to the idea that inquiry should largely follow established paths (even if to improve upon, refute, or replace them), which I associate with the idea that reality preexists and persists essentially unchanged by inquiry.

Earlier, I asserted that a widespread assumption concerning the conventional idea of knowledge at its most fundamental level exists and that it involves a characterization of a relationship between intellect and preexistent reality. This assumption is that intellect is a thing that seeks to explain the behavior of things and problems that are "already there," whether they are thought to preexist with or without human involvement. The aim of modern inquiry is to re-create reality in the form of an explanation of the way something is independent of the knower. I further claimed that scientific study of things that are thought to exist independent of human involvement is often given paradigmatic stature on the basis that it produces objective, "real" knowledge. If this characterization of the relationship is the core of the modern idea of inquiry, and if this relationship cannot be transcended, then the aim is to resituate this relationship in a way that does not limit inquiry a priori to it.

In earlier chapters, I showed that both modern visions of inquiry, and implications that I derived from postmodern critiques, place emphasis on the value of being engaged in the activity or actual experience of inquiry. The knowledge that conventional inquiry aims for is some reasoned explanation of the behavior or structure of phenomena that are experienced in the encounter. Moreover, a good explanation is one that explains not only the behavior of the phenomena that is encountered in one experience of the phenomena, but also explains the behavior of that kind of phenomena that can be expected to occur under conditions similar to those that existed in the particular experience.

Of particular significance is the idea that the object that is experienced is independent of the inquiry. The idea that reality is independent of the inquiry implies, among other things, that reality is something that is not simply transparent to the inquirer who experiences it. The independence of the object is manifested in a direct, immediate experience of it. In this kind of experience, the object is unexamined by intellect. Left unexamined, it is experienced to be independent of the inquirer (even if it is thought to be constituted by the encounter). Its independence is experienced as impenetrable, as being at an unfathomable distance, to an intellect that seeks to know things. For the inquirer, this state is an experience of indeterminacy, and it is not the desired state. In this condition, the inquirer is not where he or she wants to be, because the inquirer wants to know the object. In this sense, the inquirer is not autonomous of the object.

The desired condition is a state in which the object becomes known. An explanation of the object by the inquirer can be thought of as an attempt to overcome the autonomy that the object appears to manifest in an unexamined experience of it. An explanation is, more generally, the achievement of a new relationship with the object, one in which the object is determined. In this determination, the intellect moves from state of indeterminacy with the object to a state of determinacy, and a state in which intellect has gained autonomy relative to the object. More generally, one could think of an explanation as an effort to use objects in order to move ahead of them and gain autonomy. In the movement from a relationship of indeterminacy to determinacy, the inquirer moves outside of the immediate experience of the object to a position that is independent of the relationship that existed in the immediate experience(s) of it.

Further, this process by which the inquirer changes its relationship with the object is a movement from familiarity to unfamiliarity in the following sense. The unexamined experience of the object can be thought of as familiar in that it is commonplace for people to simply experience (and use) reality as it appears to be without analyzing it (or what philosophers often refer to as ordinary experience). Ordinary experience is the given reality that intellect seeks to determine by explanation. To make an explanation of the object is to render the object unfamiliar in that it takes the object out of its given, commonplace state and places it in a different state. In this sense, an explanation is the defamiliarization of reality. In Rorty's (and Kuhn's) terms, it renders the object abnormal.

Earlier, I stated that the conventional idea of a theory is that it is essentially a re-creation of reality—that since a theory is about some aspect of reality that is thought to be essentially autonomous in that it precedes theory, a good theory is considered to be essentially a human re-creation of reality in the form of an explanation of the way something is independent of the knower. Under the characterization of the relationship between intellect and reality that I have now introduced, a theory can just as well be understood as a means of creating reality; it is not a wholly independent reality, but nonetheless a significantly different reality from the unexamined kind. Two features of this created reality are that it is generalized and abstracted from the reality of unexamined experience. These two features are related. Generalizing two or more particular experiences or events is an act of abstraction because it rationally emphasizes aspects of the experiences that are similar and rationally de-emphasizes aspects that are dissimilar—the most basic of which is the fact that they are different experiences. To create a reality by inquiry means to make reality general.

Yet it is not apparent that this movement toward generalization and abstraction should come to a halt with explanation. I proposed above that an explanation is the achievement of a new relationship with the object, one in which the object is determined. The idea of inquiry as an intellectual activity that aims for explanation can be considered as one instance or kind of inquiry that falls under a more general concept, namely, the idea of inquiry as a determination of reality. Or, to recall a concept that I introduced in my analysis of Foucault's critique, one can think of explanation as one way for intellect to act upon reality in order to change it.

Before proceeding further, I want to emphasize two points regarding the scope of my analysis. First, I do not intend to limit this description to the kinds of phenomena and inquiries that are engaged in by empirical scientists. I mean for this description to apply to conventional inquiry in general. For example, a scholarly biographer of a writer aims to reasonably explain the writer generally by drawing conclusions from analyses of the writer's work and information from the writer's life and time as evidenced in letters, diaries, the accounts of others, and the writer's own accounts. In this inquiry, the various documents, and the various ideas expressed in them, are particular experiences that the inquirer has with reality, from which the inquirer aims to draw general explanations of who this writer really is or was, as a person and as a writer.

Second, I do not intend to limit this description to the kinds of inquiries that stress inductive methodologies. For example, a mathematician or logician who seeks to solve a problem deductively can be characterized as attempting to explain the behavior of the particular phenomena that he or she encounters, and to do so in a way that is generalizable. In short, by the words "phenomena," "reality," or "object," I mean to include things or events that are usually thought to be independent of the inquirer in some basic sense, regardless of whether these things or events are considered to be empirical formal, ideal, or to fall under some other basic category.

THE EXPERIENCE OF INTELLECTUALLY COMPELLING IDEAS

If an explanation is considered in this way, what does it mean for the task of this chapter, which is to propose a foundation for inquiry that would make room for inquiries that are not grounded in the idea of preexistent reality? Thus far, I have analyzed the problem in terms of a relationship between inquirer and reality, in which intellect moves from a place of unexamined familiarity with the object to a state in which the object is examined and rendered unfamiliar. How can this concept be used as a basis for an alternative foundation for inquiry?

An explanation is the endpoint of an inquiry. For an inquiry to take place, including the formation of a hypothesis, there is initially an experience of an unexplicated, thus unfamiliar, idea of reality, a new apprehension of the way things may be. The inchoate idea or thought may be the beginnings of an explanation, or of a new question or problem, or of the possible solution of a preexisting problem. The significance of the idea is that the initiation of an inquiry is dependent upon a decision by the inquirer of whether or not the idea is worth pursuing. Now if a good explanation, which is the end of a successful inquiry of preexisting reality, is an instance of a broader notion, the determination of reality, then an analogous notion for that which serves as precedent for the inquiry, the experience of an idea, would situate ideas of preexistent reality within a more general concept.

To formulate such a concept requires that the criteria for the decision whether to engage in an inquiry cannot be limited to whether or not the preceding idea has the potential to lead inquiry down a path to explanation of preexisting reality. What general concept can be inferred about the decision to initiate inquiry, from the concept that inquiry is initiated if it is believed that pursuit of the idea may yield such an explanation? In conventional terms, the idea must be one that, in the opinion of the inquirer, may lead the inquirer down a path that will produce new knowledge for that inquirer. An inchoate idea worth pursuing is one that suggests to the inquirer that, if pursued, it may lead to the production of new knowledge. By "new knowledge," I mean the achievement of a connection between an explanation and the phenomena. Specifically, I am thinking of three possible cases. The connection can be any of the following: (1) the application of an existing explanation to newly discovered phenomena; (2) the creation of a new explanation for already known phenomena; or (3) the creation of a new explanation to account for newly discovered phenomena.

If explanation is one instance of a more general concept of determination, then the decision whether to pursue an idea is dependent on an assessment of whether the idea may lead to a new determination of reality. I proposed above that a determination of reality is, among other things, a movement from familiarity to unfamiliarity. What role does this proposition have in regard to the decision whether to pursue a new idea?

I propose that an idea worth pursuing is, more generally, an idea whose unfamiliarity strikes the inquirer, or group of inquirers, as *intellectually compelling*. By this statement, I mean a number of things as follows. The unfamiliarity of the idea (1) interests the inquirer enough to pursue the idea, because (2) its potential difference from what the inquirer already knows suggests to that inquirer that if it is pursued, (3) it may provide the inquirer with a valuable intellectual experience.

The value of the experience that I am referring to here has at least four dimensions. First, I mean the worth of the actual engagement of a particular inquiry to the inquirer. Second, I mean the enhancement of the inquirer's capacity to form and pursue meaningful intellectual experiences as a consequence of the experience. Third, I mean the potential of the idea, or of the inquiry, to serve as the basis for other intellectually compelling inquiries, for both the inquirer and others. Fourth, I mean the potential value of the idea, inquiry, or results to be useful in application toward enhancing the quality of human experience in general (which may include quantitative factors, such as, for example, length of human life).

The fact that the idea is potentially different from what the inquirer already knows reflects that the idea and prior knowledge are related. The idea would not have occurred but for the experience that the inquirer brings to the encounter. (Indeed, it may turn out that the idea is not really different in a compelling way, but is only a restatement of what is already known.) The inquirer's previous experience and prior knowledge are not limited to the knowledge that the inquirer has experienced in a scholarly, professional capacity. It includes the gamut of life experiences, planned and accidental, large and small, that the inquirer brings to inquiry, consciously or otherwise. This account simply reflects that the occurrence of an idea, and whether the idea strikes an inquirer as potentially valuable enough to invest the effort to pursue it, are not universal, but emerge based on the particular experiences and knowledge of the inquirer(s), and their interaction with the particular idea. "Interaction" signifies that when the inquirer engages in intellectual activity, his or her intellect acts upon and works with something, apparently not identical to it, the difference of which can be approached as a problem to solve, but is more generally something to act upon, work with, and ultimately, determine.

The characteristic of difference is also intended to emphasize that the interaction of ideas that are unlike one another can be productive. However, not every idea that is different from prior knowledge stimulates an inquiry. Further, the unfamiliarity of the idea may, but does not have to, be so utterly unfamiliar that the experience it leads toward could result in what Rorty calls the "remaking" of the inquirer. Remaking is possible, but it is certainly not a necessary requirement for an idea to be unfamiliar in the way that I mean.

With this concept of the intellectually compelling idea that initiates an inquiry, the alternative description of explanation that I have proposed can be articulated further. It is not reality that is being explained in the course of an inquiry. Rather, it is the idea that was compelling enough to the particular inquirer(s) that an inquiry was initiated. The explanation of the idea yields a new determination of reality that is manifested in the term "new knowledge." Reality is that which is worked with, including material objects as well as ideas, in the production of new knowledge. Further, since a determination of reality is the achievement of autonomy relative to the object, a successful inquiry is the achievement of a new position for the inquirer relative to reality.

THE ALTERATION OF REALITY BY THE PRODUCTION OF KNOWLEDGE

The production of knowledge is also the creation of a new reality. However, this reality is never entirely new and it is not necessarily universal. It is a consequence of an interaction between a particular intellect or intellects, their experiences, and the realities that are given before them, whether they are ordinary experience or received scholarship. Existing knowledge is something to penetrate, break down, and put together in intellectually compelling ways that produce new realities and that may lead to new paths of inquiry. I will use the term "alteration of reality" to indicate that new knowledge and new realities are not wholly new, but emerge in a displacement of them by intellect. Pursuit of an intellectually compelling idea, and the production of new knowledge as a result, is the means by which reality may be altered by intellect. Further, the alteration of reality involved is contextual. A context is a way of getting into a given reality; it is composed of the assumptions and predispositions that an inquirer carries into an encounter with reality, and that make it possible to give particular form to the flux of experience and thoughts.

What does the concept of intellectually compelling ideas have to do with modern inquiry? A basic claim of the last chapter was that the pursuit of pre-existent reality dominates modern inquiry. Yet inquirers do not limit their study of thought only to those ideas of preexistent reality that are true according to contemporary criteria. Rather, accounts of preexistent reality, old and recent, attract the inquirer's interest because they vary from the particular scholar's beliefs in unfamiliar ways. Even where there are substantial similarities between contemporary thought and the thought of the past, when the latter is intellectually compelling it is because it involves similar perceptions of at least one differently situated thinker (the earlier inquirer). What Rorty and Lyotard are trying to say, using rather volatile language like "abnormal" and "paralogical" that tends to instill indignation among scholars, is that an idea that is worth thinking about is an idea that differs, or departs, from the ideas that an inquirer experienced before in such a way that it attracts intellectual curiosity. The idea is a clearing from the constraint of thinking that repeats what it already knows. It makes it possible to depart from what the inquirer already knows in order to have new intellectual experiences. It provides a way for one to think outside the bounds of one's present thought, in and to a place that is not already familiar.

The modern notion of progress obscures and unnecessarily limits the dynamic interaction between intellect and idea. The concept of modern progress adds the requirement that there is some tangible, comprehensive understanding that finally explains reality as it really is, that "gets it right," and that inquirers are trying, individually and collectively, to move toward, even if a modern position may reject the view that this understanding will ever be realized someday, and even if this aim is not directly relevant to the particular theoretical, methodological, and practical decisions that are made by inquirers in their work. The idea should be a particular contribution toward an ever-growing body of comprehensive knowledge that approximately mirrors a preexistent reality. Although reality may be dynamic and complex, it is fundamentally unified and is in principle, knowable as such in terms of explanations, large and small (including fundamental explanations of how reality changes, such as evolutionary theories). Specifically, modern progress injects the belief that an intellectually compelling idea has to be couched in terms of knowledge of reality according to some discipline-based criteria in order for it to be a legitimate intellectual idea. In this way, modern progress complicates and constrains the relationship of previous ideas to contemporary inquiry. The former have to be the true building blocks of the latter to be meaningful. Otherwise, they are the mistakes of the past, above which the metanarrative of progress distinguishes itself, thus justifying its status as the essential foundation of intellectual activity.

DISCIPLINES AS COMPELLING IDEAS AND OVERDETERMINED REALITIES

With the foregoing concepts in mind, I will now interpret the idea of a discipline in a way that removes its essentialism and recasts it as a particular intellectually compelling idea. To understand the intellectually compelling quality of the disciplines, one must understand: (1) the compelling quality of knowledge of preexistent reality, and (2) the compelling quality of the disciplines in terms of knowledge of preexistent reality. For the ancient Greeks, the striking difference of the idea of knowledge of reality was its difference from myth. What struck Greek intellect is the idea that there is an inherent, intimate connection between the human being and an enduring reality on the basis of reason, rather than a relationship that is understood in terms of myth. The striking quality of knowledge was the idea that this enduring reality is accessible to human reason. For this reason, Aristotle could speak of the pursuit of knowledge as being "its own end." On this basis, the ancients could meaningfully connect the idea of knowledge of reality with the idea of how to live. Access to reality through intellect meant that the human being could live with reality as a fundamental part of it. The idea of knowledge of reality also struck the ancient intellect as a diversity that human reason could access and categorize in a way that yielded a comprehensive understanding of reality. This understanding would be the means of informing the human being of its proper place and purpose in the order of reality.

The predominant form of this categorization is the disciplinary matrix. The intellectually compelling quality of the idea of each discipline is twofold. First, the idea of a discipline is the idea of a unique and basic form and category of knowledge of an enduring reality that is accessible through reason. Second, the intellectually compelling quality of the idea of a discipline is that it is a complementary part of the whole of reality. On these bases, each discipline is accorded the status of its object, an enduring reality.

The compelling quality of a new idea within a discipline is that it suggests explanations of (1) what is true of reality in terms of the discipline that the idea falls within, and/or (2) how to know reality in terms of that discipline. Since the evidence is discipline-bound, the enduring object of knowledge is a disciplinary object. A person who has a proper understanding has an understanding that conforms with the way a disciplinary object "really is," whether that object is believed to be real, ideal, or formal, or knowable objectively, subjectively, or intersubjectively.

The modern idea of disciplines attempts to accommodate the practical fact that intellectually compelling ideas are not always susceptible of falling neatly within any existing discipline's criteria for knowledge. That is, modern inquiry seeks to accommodate the fact that intellect persistently seeks to express compelling ideas that cannot be proven, or even articulated, according to the criteria that are established in the disciplinary matrix as that matrix is given at any point in time. Thus, modern inquiry allows new disciplines to appear on occasion (sometimes replacing existing disciplines), and subdisciplines much more often (the explosion of the latter relative to the former is an indication of the practical hold of established disciplines). The parameters of what constitutes intellectually compelling ideas are ideas that are known to be true in disciplinary terms. On this basis, the disciplines have maintained the intellectual status of the object that ultimately grounds them, knowledge of an enduring reality.

However, from the perspective developed here, the idea that knowledge is a true and justified belief of an enduring reality is only one particular intellectually compelling idea. If so, then the disciplines can be construed to be something other than complementary parts of a generally coherent, enduring matrix that progresses collectively toward a better representation of an enduring reality or realities. Individually, each discipline can be thought of as particular contexts, or ways of getting into and working with reality, that is, as constellations of particular alterations of reality. These constellations are composed of the particular assumptions and predispositions that an inquirer may choose from in order to give particular form to the flux of experience and thoughts. As a whole, the disciplines can be thought of as composing a particular constellation of contexts, grounded on the idea of preexisting reality. In this case, the essentialism of the disciplines is unjustified, because they are not general grounds, but only particular intellectually compelling ideas.

If these ideas are an unnecessary constraint on intellect, how can this constraint be usefully described in terms of the inquirer's desired condition, namely, a state in which the object becomes determined by the inquirer, who thereby gains autonomy relative to the object? The constraint is that explaining reality in terms of preexistence is only one particular way of determining reality. For this reason, the domination of disciplinary inquiry has become largely overdetermined relative to the inquirer, even if the disciplines yield new, compelling ideas of preexisting reality. By "overdetermination," I refer to the predominance of this kind of inquiry of reality, in that it largely shapes how intellect conceives inquiry, reality, and inquirer in a way that is excessively and unnecessarily disproportionate, if one understands the disciplines as only particular ideas.

This overdetermination is manifest in at least three ways. First, it is manifest in the fact that the disciplines ground inquiry generally. Second, inquirers are required to specialize in a discipline in order to be considered fit to engage in legitimate inquiry. Third, the undergraduate curriculum, despite its increasing breadth and variety of permutations in different institutions, remains essentially disciplinary. An implicit assumption that I make here is that the intellectual capacities of scholars evident in their abilities to think at exquisite orders of complexity, and of potential scholars, is unnecessarily underdeveloped by the a priori requirement that inquiry be essentially about preexisting reality. In effect, the disciplines are the preexisting reality that an alternative foundation for inquiry must act upon.

CONSEQUENCES: THE INQUIRER AS CAUSE

What are the consequences of viewing the disciplines as local contexts of one particular compelling idea, namely, the idea of a preexistent and enduring reality? If knowledge of reality is a particular intellectually compelling idea, then inquiry does not have to be grounded in disciplines. Inquiry can be expressly altered by other considerations. For example, an inquiry can be altered in ways that go beyond the effort to arrange words and objects to accurately represent or explain reality. To distinguish this form of inquiry from inquiries based in disciplines, interdisciplinary work, and applied fields, I will use the phrase "postdisciplinary inquiry."

To specify what postdisciplinary inquiry would be in detail would be inconsistent with the postmodern critique of modern inquiry because it would impose another preexisting reality on inquiry before it has been undertaken. Nevertheless, if the ideas that generate any inquiry arises from the raw material of previous inquiries, thoughts, experiences, and reflections, it is possible to provide an indication of what postdisciplinary inquiry could entail.

Outside the disciplines, words and objects that have been arranged to produce knowledge within the disciplines would be rearranged to produce intellectually compelling inquiries that are not about explaining preexisting reality. Rather, they would be about what reality could become. Inquiry, thus conceived, would bring together ideas that, from particular standpoints within the disciplines, do not belong together as consistent parts of a disciplinary language or of a cross-disciplinary language. From the standpoint of modern inquiry, these alternative constellations may appear to be disparate, paradoxical, or even a-logical and a-rational arrangements. However, disparity or paradox ends inquiry only if one insists on limiting inquiry to the pursuit of preexistent reality. Similarly, what is a-logical or a-rational intellectual activity is not predetermined for any particular inquiry.

Justification for this kind of intellectual activity is that the overall fragmented condition of knowledge is normal. The contemporary fragmentation of knowledge is not an abnormality to be overcome by unifying its pursuit in accord with the idea of a unified reality. Fragmentation is the consequence of the ultimate inaccessibility of reality, and the concomitant context-dependence of any inquiry. It reflects the disconnected, particularistic nature of contemporary inquiry, and the emphasis on producing new knowledge, on overcoming the autonomy of the object, rather than on unifying knowledge. However, fragmentation within the disciplines and the blurring of disciplinary boundaries are only particular ways that this condition can be manifested.

Fragmentation results from two conflicting and unresolvable intellectual desires: the desire to have a comprehensive knowledge of reality that unifies the diversity of its particulars, and the desire to subject knowledge to doubt so that intellect can create different, intellectually compelling explanations of reality. In a sense, postdisciplinary inquiry is an implication of this intellectual condition of having to pursue, yet having to doubt. Such inquiry would make explicit what modern inquiry obscures: that the pursuit of knowledge ultimately has to reject what is given in order to think about reality in intellectually compelling ways. Fragmentation also means at least in part that the course of knowledge is not stable because stability is not finally satisfactory to intellect. Intellect desires to be active without the requirement that it must do so within the context of one particular idea, the idea that reality preexists inquiry and persists essentially unchanged by it.

Postdisciplinary inquiry would make this tacit modern desire explicit so that the capacity of intellect can be released from the domination of this particular idea. Rather than attempting simply to repair fragmentation, as if the disorder of the university is a congeries of abnormalities to be fixed, mediated, or ignored, these inquiries would work with the myriad of fragments, reconceived as local contexts, to defamiliarize and reshape them in ways that produce new, intellectually compelling alterations of reality.

The pursuit of preexistent reality is fueled by a desire to depart from the given. The original departure, the departure of the ancient Greeks, is a departure from *mythos* to *logos*, from unreasoned determinations to reasoned determinations. Subsequent departures of modern *logos* have tended to be movements "toward" the enduring object: efforts to get closer and closer to the way aspects of reality "really are," behind the veil of familiarity. In contrast, postdisciplinary inquiry is partly a movement beyond the idea of an enduring object. This departure does not mean that it is a flight from reason, unless the assumption is made that intellect already knows what the parameters of reason are before an inquiry is experienced.

Postdisciplinary inquiry approaches disciplinary knowledge as something to experience in unfamiliar and compelling ways. To do this would mean to experience ideas not as objects that represent reality but rather as themselves constituting preexisting realities of autonomous objects to be determined and overcome by inquiry. The diverse products of the rich pursuit of preexistent reality are things to use in order to go beyond them with the aim of altering reality in other compelling ways. The aim of postdisciplinary inquiry generally would be to extend the capacity of intellect to create new realities. It would not be constrained by the assumptions and methods of particular disciplines or particular forms of inquiry; instead, it creates possibilities for inquiry, both within and outside disciplines. Disparate ideas would not be brought together to resolve or unify them. Rather, they would be bounced off of one another to create new contexts as starting points for inquiry, starting points that use, instead of follow, what is already there—to create new determinations of reality.

From the standpoint of postdisciplinary inquiry, disciplinary knowledge is not to be built upon but used to create new inquiries. The past, namely, the results of previous inquiries, would be brought into the present act and rearranged, rather than extended, improved upon, or refuted. Past discoveries are ideas to bring into being in the present intellectual experience, to be used to change the present by the creation of compelling inquiries. In a sense, the *paths* of inquiry are the knowledge that is produced, and it is knowledge to be experienced, and in the course of experience, changed and used differently. Objects of knowledge are points along the way.

A new context for inquiry could emerge by borrowing particular elements or parts of existing theories and methods, or whole theories or methods, or by creating new elements using particular elements as metaphors, or by any combination of these approaches. Even ideas that would be considered outmoded from current disciplinary vantage points could be used in this way, rather than being mere building blocks or mistakes. The history of ideas would be seen not as constituting a continuum but rather a multidimensional collage.

Since disciplinary boundaries are predicated on an assumption that I analyzed earlier, namely, a relationship between intellect as a thing that seeks to know preexistent reality and reality as that which is already there, and on the assumption that inquiry is the study of reality so conceived, the postmodern blurring of these boundaries means that the boundary between reality and its representation in the form of theoretical knowledge is also blurred. Reality becomes something that is produced in the course of inquiry rather than an object that is essentially separate from the inquiry and that inquiry seeks to discover, accurately represent, and explain. In this sense, knowledge of reality is an irreducible combination of intellectual activity and the things that intellect works with, including language, ideas, and material objects.

In a broader sense, disciplinary and postdisciplinary inquiry would compose a two-way interaction between particular inquiries within disciplines and ideas outside of them. Ideas outside the disciplines impact what knowledge of reality can mean and the ways in which knowledge of reality is pursued, while the latter provide the raw material for the construction of compelling ideas that cut across the disciplines. In this way, each side continuously affects the nature of the other. In both cases, reality is something to work with and act upon, a condition to be determined in inquiry. The disciplines and applied fields would remain places where the pursuit of preexisting realities is carried out. Further, they would serve as a primary source of ideas for postdisciplinary inquiry to use. However, they would not be structures within which new inquiries would have to fit. What would be removed is the essential, a priori status of the disciplinary plane.

Further, it is possible that postdisciplinary inquiry could influence the nature of, and even commingle with, inquiry within the disciplines and applied fields. In this case, the distinction between preexisting, persistent realities, on one hand, and other, postdisciplinary realities, on the other, would itself be "rearranged." New forms of organization for inquiry could emerge that would not necessarily be fundamentally distinguished on the basis of subject matter. Instead, they could be composed of forms of thought that emerge in the course of particular inquiries that have points of compatibility and thus can serve as links across such inquiries. These forms would be dynamic, temporary networks of linkages that provide intellectual guides for thinkers to orient their thought amid the flux of ideas. They would always be potentially subject to change, dissolution, and replacement as different linkages emerge and networks are reconfigured. These discipline-networks would manage the flux of particular pursuits of knowledge so that particulars can inform each other for the purpose of creating new lines of inquiry and new linkages rather than establishing themselves as general explanations.

The alternative foundation that the foregoing analysis points toward is one that is *inquirer-based* rather than object-based. In modern inquiry, the object takes precedence, in that intellectual activity is focused on determining the object as it really is, that is, as an entity that exists before and independent of the inquiry, and that persists essentially unchanged by the inquiry. The object is the locus of causal explanation. Assumptions, methods, and procedures are aimed at capturing, in the form of theoretical explanation, this preexistent object as such.

In contrast, the foundation advocated here places precedence on the inquirer as an active agent who causes knowledge to be created, and reality to thereby change. The precedence on the inquirer applies to both disciplinary and postdisciplinary inquiries. In both cases, the inquirer makes decisions about how to encounter reality before and during an inquiry, by choosing subject matter, theories, methods, and procedures. At the first, disciplinary, level, these decisions are based on the pursuit of preexisting reality. At this level, the history of ideas is approached as a continuum in which knowledge of reality progresses over time. The baseline reality of immediate experience is overcome by reconstituting it in terms that are outside immediate experience and initially unfamiliar. The aim is to explain reality, which is assumed to exist before and independent of inquiry, and to persist essentially unchanged by the inquiry.

At the second, postdisciplinary, level, disciplinary knowledge is the baseline, overdetermined reality to be overcome. Inquiry moves outside the experience of disciplinary reality in terms that are initially unfamiliar. Decisions are made in order to rearrange the realities of the disciplines by engaging in inquiries that move beyond them to explore what reality can become. At this level, inquiry cuts across the preexisting reality, established knowledge and the history of ideas is reconstituted as a multidimensional collage. The aim of inquiry is to *explore* rather than to explain reality, for the purpose of enhancing human experience.

The underlying principle of both levels is that the basis for an inquiry is a context chosen by the inquirer for the purpose of initiating an interaction between inquirer and that which is apparently not identical to the inquirer, in order to pursue the experience of an intellectually compelling idea. The pursuit of preexisting reality is only one particular compelling form, and contexts for inquiry are not rationally constrained to it. The choice of subject matter, theories, methods, and procedures does not have to be grounded in the idea of preexisting reality. Contexts can be composed of ideas that are not, from a modern perspective, compatible.

POSTDISCIPLINARY RESEARCH PROGRAMS

What form could postdisciplinary inquiry take as an intellectual activity? How would this second level be organized to cut across disciplinary reality? It would have to be free-standing, in the sense of not being contained within, or itself constitute, permanent structures. Second, it would have to be fluid and mobile in order to locate and work with disciplinary disparities. Specifically, it would have to be a form of inquiry in which both the subject and object of the inquiry would be the evolving experience of the inquiry itself.

I will call this institutional form of intellectual activity postdisciplinary research programs. A postdisciplinary research program would be composed of two or more scholars from disparate disciplines who choose to affiliate with the aim of pursuing an intellectually compelling idea or ideas that are not about preexisting reality. Research programs would not be bound by disciplinary boundaries or by established cross-disciplinary compatibilities in the pursuit of compelling ideas. Members of a program would explore the ways that their respective disciplines and/or applied fields could be used to rearrange preexisting reality in order to generate compelling new lines of inquiry.

The disparity across disciplinary approaches within a program would be used as the basis for moving inquiry beyond disciplinary constraints in the course of pursuing the idea. In effect, the disciplines would be the raw material for the pursuit of forms of reasoning that would not be constrained by established disciplinary and interdisciplinary structures and boundaries. Modern disciplines would then function as points of departure for new paths of thought rather than top-down a priori structures that largely determine the nature and course of particular inquiries.

Further, two or more research programs could affiliate for the mutual purpose of pursuing compelling interactions of ideas. The perpetuation of a research program or affiliation would be a function of its capacity to generate compelling new ideas. The fluidity of research programs would discourage the entrenchment of ideas. In effect, a vital and/or flexible program would itself be in a state of ongoing transformation.

Equally important, since the distinction between research and teaching is associated with the idea of knowledge as something one pursues to have, and then transmit, the distinction between research and teaching would become blurred within postdisciplinary research programs. Knowledge, research, and teaching would be considered practically inseparable aspects of activity. Postdisciplinary research programs would be places of instruction as well as research. Teaching would become integral to research rather than essentially the after-the-fact transmission of its results. Teaching would not be something one does in addition to or instead of research but something one does through and in the course of research. Research would become a means of teaching rather than an end in itself. Thus, portions of both graduate and undergraduate curricula would emerge from postdisciplinary research. Since research programs would be dynamic and flexible rather than accumulative and progressive, curricula could change nearly as often as new inquiries. Indeed, the relationship between this "live" curriculum and faculty research programs would be two-way, since compelling ideas could emerge in the classroom and affect the course of faculty research.

ANTICIPATION OF INQUIRER AS CAUSE

The critiques of modern inquiry of Lyotard, Rorty, Schrag, Foucault, and Derrida can be understood to anticipate postdisciplinary inquiry. Derrida, Rorty, and Schrag work outside philosophy and literature, Foucault works outside philosophy and history, and Lyotard works outside science and history. Further, these five critiques, particularly those of the three French philosophers are not only "about" an alternative idea of inquiry; they are exercises of it. Are there other examples of recent vintage that anticipate postdisciplinary inquiry? What do these examples mean if they are given an expanded interpretation, one that emphasizes the inquirer as a cause of reality? A full explication of the connection between postdisciplinary inquiry and examples of the various strands of modern inquiry is beyond the scope of this inquiry. However, I will cite several examples to give an indication of that postdisciplinary inquiry that alters preexisting reality is anticipated by some current trends.

In the discipline of philosophy, over the past thirty years, numerous challenges to the pursuit of ahistorical foundations for science and knowledge have emerged through significant critiques within the philosophy of science, notably represented by Paul Feyerabend, Mary Hesse, Thomas Kuhn, Imre Lakatos, and Karl Popper, and by analytic epistemologists and philosophers of language, notably represented by Richard Rorty, Stanley Cavell, Nelson Goodman, Jack Meiland, Hilary Putnam, and W. V. O. Quine.[2] A sociology of scientific inquiry influenced by the work of Kuhn and others has also emerged, notably at the hands of Michael Mulkay and the British school of sociology of science.[3]

Kuhn's idea of scientific revolutions as foundation-altering paradigm shifts and Feyerabend's critique of method, to cite two important critiques of conventional philosophy of science and scientific method, can be given expanded interpretations that do not imply a diminution of the pursuit of scientific knowledge.[4] From the perspective that I have introduced here, the significance of these ideas is unduly diminished if one understands them as being essentially critiques of objectivistic science. More importantly, they can be understood as manifestations of the desire by intellect to enlarge the opportunity for scholars to pursue inquiries that depart from the disciplinary plane without removing it. They are indications that intellect is seeking in part to get out of the confines of preexisting reality and the disciplines, toward forms of inquiry that provide the inquirer with much more latitude to actively shape and pursue compelling ideas that are not limited by these confines.

Further, some of the pictures of reality that have emerged from scientific inquiry itself over the past one hundred years suggest that reality is much less objective and unified than the "project of modernity" has tended to assume, such that an inquirer-based concept of inquiry is more appropriate than the prevailing object-based one. An important example that stems from quantum physics is that, from an empirical standpoint, the question of whether an observer-independent reality is fundamentally knowable may be problematic.[5] Another illustrative example is current work in cognitive learning theory in psychology, particularly the shift from learning as the acquisition of existing organized knowledge intact, to learning as effective knowledge utilization and the meaningful transformation, reorganization, and clarification of ideas.[6] Further, the work of psychologist Howard Gardner emphasizes broadening how human cognition is conceived beyond logical problem-solving and orderly, rule-governed analysis.[7] Perhaps the strand of inquiry that has the most explicit connection to an inquirer-based idea of inquiry places the reader as an active creator of texts rather than being a recipient of it.[8] This idea blurs the distinction between writer and reader. One particularly promising approach utilizes the flexibility and power of computer technology to create new forms of expression called hypertext and hypermedia.[9]

An area of current research in a number of disciplines and fields, among them biology, computer science, economics, mathematics, physics, political science, that can be understood to anticipate an inquirer-based model of inquiry and postdisciplinary forms of inquiry is known as complexity theory.[10] These inquiries attempt to understand systems as spontaneous, adaptive, and self-organizing entities that mediate between order and disorder by systemwide transformations. Like the other areas of inquiry that I have mentioned here, complexity theory is largely understood as a new scientific explanation. In this case, the claim is that it is a more accurate way of understanding the behavior of natural and artificial systems than theories that assume fundamental stability because theoretically, it accounts for the observed instability of systems as well. However, if complexity is given an expanded interpretation, its significance is in application to postdisciplinary inquiry. The emphasis placed on adaptation to changing circumstances, spontaneity, and transformation is compatible with the postdisciplinary concepts of dynamism, alteration, and interaction. Most important, one could think of a postdisciplinary research program as a complex, open system within which the inquirers are active parts rather than being observers of stable, preexisting disciplinary realities. The inquirers' function would be serve as agents or causes of the disorganization and subsequent reorganization of otherwise stable discipline-based concepts.

Qualitative theories and methods are another example of current research that can be understood to anticipate postdisciplinary inquiry.[11] In particular, the idea that the researcher chooses methods in the course of the inquiry as their utility becomes apparent, rather than before the inquiry, and that the course of the research process may be essentially constructed in the process are applicable to postdisciplinary research programs. For example, inquiry can be composed of a local constellation of contexts using particular pieces of existing theories as metaphors for new pursuits.

Expanding the realm of what counts as legitimate inquiry does not entail a denial that some aspects of reality, at least, are objective and knowable as such. However, these intellectual currents do suggest that the idea of an inquiry is much less a function of the object and much more a function of practice. The essential difference between these currents and postdisciplinary inquiry is that the former are generally about preexisting reality. The proposal made here is that they can be reasonably interpreted to be more than new or better ways of knowing preexisting reality. Though they are not explicitly about postdisciplinary inquiry, they can be usefully interpreted to anticipate it.

THE BASIS FOR INTELLECTUAL COMMUNITY

If the alternative foundation for inquiry that I have proposed here does not advocate a unified reality to know, what happens to the idea that scholars belong to an intellectual community? If there is no whole to permanently establish, if inquiry is local, does the desire to not be constrained to improving or bettering received knowledge mean a rejection of intellectual community?

There is no good reason why an intellectual community has to be dependent on the idea of preexisting reality. Intellectual community can be more usefully thought of as something that is continually being made in the activity of inquiry. The preexisting reality of received knowledge can be thought of as something to freely use as well as to build upon. However, the ground of this activity would be the communal experience of intellectually compelling ideas rather than the progressive accumulation of discoveries.

Both within and outside the disciplines, postmodern intellect would seek to produce compelling ideas with the aim of communicating them. Intellectual community would be the perpetuation of this dynamic communicative activity in specific encounters between individuals. The emphasis on exploration as well as explanation, on the creation of postdisciplinary paths, and on crossing divergent ideas and disciplinary affiliations suggests that the basis for this new community would be the engagement of intellectual activity, rather than the acquisition of similar knowledge of objects.

In this community, an inquirer would be part of something larger than itself in that (1) the desire to have compelling intellectual experiences is common across scholars, (2) this desire is not accomplished without using the ideas of others to produce new compelling ideas, and (3) the experience is ultimately consummated with realization of the desire to share the new idea in order to enhance the possibility of new intellectually compelling ideas. The community progresses in the sense that the capacity of intellect to work with ever-more complex concepts and alterations of existing ideas is enhanced over time resulting from more experience engaging in increasingly complex intellectual activity.

The value of the ideas that this community generates would not have to be grounded in a presumption that on balance, they are liable to result in the advancement of society as a fundamentally unified whole. They could create new forms of human activity that directly enhance the quality of human experience beyond the university, not only in principle but in actuality.

A great deal of modern research is motivated by a desire to enhance the welfare of other human communities, or of human society generally. However, the emphasis on explaining aspects of reality unduly constrains scholars from realizing this aim. The alternative foundation that I have proposed here would give intellect more room to move outside of the modern context toward actually altering, as well as explaining, the conditions of human experience. In this way, inquiry could have a more direct effect on the welfare of other communities. The modern pursuit of preexisting reality is only the beginning of intellectual activity, and only the beginning of proposals about what reality can mean. It is also only the beginning of what an intellectual community can be, and of what it can become for other communities.

NOTES

1. Michel Foucault, "Polemics, Politics, and Problematizations," in *The Foucault Reader*, ed. Paul Rabinow (New York: Pantheon, 1984), 390.

2. Paul Feyerabend, *Against Method* (London: New Left Books, 1977); Mary Hesse, *Revolutions and Reconstructions in the Philosophy of Science* (Brighton, England: Harvester, 1980); Thomas S. Kuhn, *The Structure of Scientific Revolutions*, 2d ed. (Chicago: University of Chicago Press, 1970); Imre Lakatos, "Falsification and the Methodology of Research Programmes," in Imre Lakatos and Alan Musgrave, eds., *Criticism and the Growth of Knowledge* (Cambridge, U. K.: Cambridge University Press, 1970); Karl Popper, *The Logic of Scientific Discovery* (London: Hutchinson, 1959); Stanley Cavell, *The Claim of Reason* (Oxford: Oxford University Press, 1979); Nelson Goodman, *Ways of Worldmaking* (Indianapolis: Hackett, 1978); Jack W. Meiland and Michael Krausz, eds., *Relativism, Cognitive and Moral* (Notre Dame: University of Notre Dame Press, 1982); Jack W. Meiland, "On the Paradox of Cognitive Relativism," *Metaphilosophy* 11, no. 2 (April 1980): 115–126; Jack W. Meiland, "Concepts of Relative Truth," *Monist* 60, no. 4 (1977): 568–582; Hilary Putnam, *Realism with a Human Face* (Cambridge, Mass.: Harvard University Press, 1990); Hilary Putnam, *Renewing Philosophy* (Cambridge, Mass.: Harvard University Press, 1992); W.V.O. Quine, *From a Logical Point of View* (Cambridge, Mass.: Harvard University Press, 1953).

3. Feyerabend, *Against Method*; Kuhn, *Scientific Revolutions*.

4. Michael Mulkay, *Science and the Sociology of Knowledge* (London: George Allen and Unwin, 1979); Michael Mulkay, *Sociology of Science: A Sociological Pilgrimage* (Bloomington: Indiana University Press, 1991).

5. For rigorous analyses of this issue, see David Park, *The How and the Why: An Essay on the Origins and Development of Physical Theory* (Princeton: Princeton University Press, 1988), chaps. 15, 16; John L. Casti, *Paradigms Lost: Tackling the Unanswered Mysteries of Modern Science* (New York: William Morrow, 1989), chap. 7.

6. Roger H. Bruning, "The College Classroom from the Perspective of Cognitive Psychology," in Keith W. Prichard and R. McLaren Sawyer, eds., *Handbook of College Teaching: Theory and Applications* (Westport: Greenwood Press, 1994), 3–22; Marilla D. Svinicki, "Practical Implications of Cognitive Theories," in Robert J. Menges and Marilla D. Svinicki, eds., *College Teaching: From Theory to Practice* (San Francisco: Jossey-Bass, 1991), 27–37; Wilbert McKeachie, Paul Pintrich, Yi-Guang Lin, and David A. F. Smith, *Teaching and Learning in the College Classroom: A Review of Research Literature* (Ann Arbor: National Center for Research to Improve Postsecondary Teaching and Learning, 1986).

7. Howard Gardner, *Frames of Mind: The Theory of Multiple Intelligences* (New York: Basic Books, 1983).

8. The seminal work in this area is Roland Barthes's *S/Z*, trans. Richard Miller (New York: Hill and Wang, 1974).

9. See George P. Landow, *Hypertext: The Convergence of Contemporary Critical Theory and Technology* (Baltimore: Johns Hopkins University Press, 1992); Michael Joyce, *Of Two Minds: Hypertext Pedagogy and Poetics* (Ann Arbor: University of Michigan Press, 1995).

10. See M. Mitchell Waldrop, *Complexity: The Emerging Science at the Edge of Order and Chaos* (New York: Simon and Schuster, 1992); John L. Casti, *Complexification: Explaining a Paradoxical World Through the Science of Surprise* (New York: Harper Collins, 1994); John H. Holland, *Hidden Order: How Adaptation Builds Complexity* (New York: Addison-Wesley, 1995).

11. An excellent source for both the history of, and current developments in, qualitative research is Norman K. Denzin and Yvonna S. Lincoln, eds., *Handbook of Qualitative Research* (Thousand Oaks, Calif.: Sage Publications, 1994).

Bibliography

Arac, Jonathan, ed. *After Foucault: Humanistic Knowledge, Postmodern Challenges.* New Brunswick, N.J.: Rutgers University Press, 1988.
Arcilla, Rene V. *For the Love of Perfection: Richard Rorty and Liberal Education.* New York: Routledge, 1995.
Aristotle. *Metaphysics.* C. A. Kirwan Clarendon Aristotle Series, 1971. Translated by W. Jaeger, Oxford Classical Texts, 1957.
Aristotle. *Nicomachean Ethics.* Translated by W. D. Ross. Revised by J. Barnes. Oxford: Oxford University Press, 1984.
Baldwin, John W. *The Scholastic Culture of the Middle Ages, 1000–1300.* Lexington, Mass.: D. C. Heath, 1971.
Ball, Stephen J., ed. *Foucault and Education: Disciplines and Knowledge.* London: Routledge, 1990.
Barthes, Roland. *The Rustle of Language.* New York: Hill and Wang, 1986.
Barthes, Roland. *S/Z.* Translated by Richard Miller. New York: Hill and Wang, 1974.
Bernauer, James W. *Michel Foucault's Force of Flight: Toward an Ethics for Thought.* Atlantic Highlands, N. J.: Humanities Press International, 1990.
Bernauer, James, and David Rasmussen, eds. *The Final Foucault.* Cambridge, Mass.: MIT Press, 1988.
Bernstein, Richard J. *Beyond Objectivism and Relativism: Science, Hermeneutics, and Praxis.* Philadelphia: University of Pennsylvania Press, 1983.
Bernstein, Richard J., ed. *Habermas and Modernity.* Cambridge, Mass.: MIT Press, 1985.
Best, Steven, and Douglas Kellner. *Postmodern Theory: Critical Interrogations.* New York: Guilford, 1991.
Bruning, Roger H. "The College Classroom from the Perspective of Cognitive Psychology." In *Handbook of College Teaching: Theory and Applications.* Edited by Keith W. Prichard and R. McLaren Sawyer. Westport: Greenwood Press, 1994, pp. 3–22.
Caputo, John, and Mark Yount, eds. *Foucault and the Critique of Institutions.* Univer-

sity Park, Pa: Pennsylvania University Press, 1993.
Casti, John L. *Complexification: Explaining a Paradoxical World Through the Science of Surprise.* New York: Harper Collins, 1994.
Casti, John L. *Paradigms Lost: Tackling the Unanswered Mysteries of Modern Science.* New York: William Morrow, 1989.
Cavell, Stanley. *The Claim of Reason.* Oxford: Oxford University Press, 1979.
Clark, Mary E., and Sandra A. Wawrytko, eds. *Rethinking the Curriculum: Toward an Integrated, Interdisciplinary College Education.* Westport, Conn.: Greenwood Press, 1990.
Cousins, Mark, and Athar Hussain. *Michel Foucault.* London: Macmillan, 1984.
Culler, Jonathan. *On Deconstruction: Theory and Criticism after Structuralism.* Ithaca: Cornell University Press, 1982.
Danto, Arthur C. *Connections to the World.* New York: Harper & Row, 1989.
Deleuze, Gilles. *Foucault.* London: Athlone, 1988.
Denzin, Norman K., and Yvonna S. Lincoln, eds. *Handbook of Qualitative Research.* Thousand Oaks, Calif.: Sage Publications, 1994.
Derrida, Jacques. *The Archeology of the Frivolous: Reading Condillac.* Translated by John P. Leavey. Lincoln: University of Nebraska Press, 1987.
Derrida, Jacques. "Canons and Metonymies: An Interview with Jacques Derrida." In *Logomachia: The Conflict of the Faculties.* Edited by Richard Rand. Lincoln: University of Nebraska, 1992, pp. 195–218.
Derrida, Jacques. "Difference." In *Speech and Phenomena and Other Essays on Husserl's Theory of Signs.* Translated by David B. Allison. Evanston: Northwestern University Press, 1973.
Derrida, Jacques. *Dissemination.* Translated by Barbara Harlow. Chicago: University of Chicago Press, 1981.
Derrida, Jacques. *Edmund Husserl's "Origin of Geometry": An Introduction.* Translated by John P. Leavey. Pittsburgh: Duquesne University Press, 1978.
Derrida, Jacques. *Glas.* Translated by John P. Leavey Jr., and Richard Rand. Lincoln: University of Nebraska Press, 1986.
Derrida, Jacques. *Of Grammatology.* Translated by Gayatri Chakravorty Spivak. Baltimore: Johns Hopkins University Press, 1976.
Derrida, Jacques. *Limited, Inc.* Baltimore: Johns Hopkins University Press, 1988.
Derrida, Jacques. *Margins of Philosophy.* Translated by Alan Bass. Chicago: University of Chicago Press, 1982.
Derrida, Jacques. "Mochlos; or, The Conflict of the Faculties." In *Logomachia: The Conflict of the Faculties.* Edited by Richard Rand. Lincoln: University of Nebraska, 1992, pp. 3–34.
Derrida, Jacques. "The Original Discussion of '*Differance*' (1968)." In *Derrida and Differance,* edited by David Wood and Robert Bernasconi. Evanston: Northwestern University Press, 1988, pp. 83–95.
Derrida, Jacques. *Positions.* Translated by Alan Bass. Chicago: University of Chicago, 1981.
Derrida, Jacques. *The Post Card: From Socrates to Freud and Beyond.* Translated by Alan Bass. Chicago: University of Chicago Press, 1987.
Derrida, Jacques. "The Principle of Reason: The University in the Eyes of its Pupils." *Diacritics* 13 (1983): 3–20.
Derrida, Jacques. *Speech and Phenomena and Other Essays on Husserl's Theory of*

Signs. Translated by David B. Allison. Evanston: Northwestern University Press, 1973.
Derrida, Jacques. *Of Spirit: Heidegger and the Question*. Translated by Geoffrey Bennington and Rachel Bowlby. Chicago: University of Chicago Press, 1989.
Derrida, Jacques. *Spurs: Nietzsche's Styles*. Translated by Barbara Harlow. Chicago: University of Chicago Press, 1979.
Derrida, Jacques. *The Truth in Painting*. Translated by Geoffrey Bennington and Ian McLeod. Chicago: University of Chicago Press, 1987.
Derrida, Jacques. *Writing and Difference*. Translated by Alan Bass. Chicago: University of Chicago Press, 1978.
Dewey, John. *Experience and Education*. New York: Collier-Macmillan, 1963. Originally published 1938.
Dreyfus, Hubert L., and Paul Rabinow. *Michel Foucault: Beyond Structuralism and Hermeneutics*. 2d ed. Chicago: University of Chicago Press, 1983.
Evans, J. Claude. *Strategies of Deconstruction: Derrida and the Myth of the Voice*. Minneapolis: University of Minnesota Press, 1991.
Feyerabend, Paul. *Against Method*. London: New Left Books, 1977.
Foster, Hal, ed. *The Anti-Aesthetic: Essays on Postmodern Culture*. Port Townsend, Wash.: Bay Press, 1983.
Foucault, Michel. *The Archaeology of Knowledge*. Translated by Alan Sheridan. New York: Harper & Row, 1976.
Foucault, Michel. *The Birth of the Clinic: An Archaeology of Medical Perception*. Translated by Alan Sheridan. New York: Random House, 1975.
Foucault, Michel. *Discipline and Punish: The Birth of the Prison*. Translated by Alan Sheridan. New York: Random House, 1979.
Foucault, Michel. *The History of Sexuality. Volume 1: An Introduction*. Translated by R. Hurley. New York: Random House, 1978.
Foucault, Michel. *The History of Sexuality. Volume 2: The Use of Pleasure*. Translated by R. Hurley. New York: Random House, 1985.
Foucault, Michel. *The History of Sexuality. Volume 3: The Care of the Self*. Translated by R. Hurley. New York: Random House, 1986.
Foucault, Michel. *Language, Counter-Memory, Practice: Selected Essays and Interviews*. Edited by Donald F. Bouchard. Ithaca: Cornell University Press, 1977.
Foucault, Michel. *Madness and Civilization: A History of Insanity in the Age of Reason*. Translated by Richard Howard. New York: Random House, 1965.
Foucault, Michel. *Michel Foucault: Power, Truth, Strategy*. Edited by M. Morris and P. Patton. Sydney: Feral, 1979.
Foucault, Michel. "Nietzsche, Genealogy, History." In *The Foucault Reader*. Edited by Paul Rabinow. New York: Pantheon, 1984, pp. 76-100.
Foucault, Michel. *The Order of Things: An Archaeology of the Human Sciences*. Translated by Alan Sheridan. London: Tavistock, 1970.
Foucault, Michel. *Power/Knowledge: Selected Interviews and Other Writings*. Edited by Colin Gordon. New York: Random House, 1980.
Foucault, Michel. "The Subject and Power." In *Michel Foucault: Beyond Structuralism and Hermeneutics*. 2d ed. Written by Hubert L. Dreyfus and Paul Rabinow. Chicago: University of Chicago Press, 1983.
Gardner, Howard. *Frames of Mind: The Theory of Multiple Intelligences*. New York: Basic Books, 1983.

Gasche, Rodolphe. *The Tain of the Mirror: Derrida and the Philosophy of Reflection.* Cambridge, Mass.: Harvard University Press, 1986.
Giamatti, A. Bartlett. *A Free and Ordered Space: The Real World of the University.* New York: W. W. Norton, 1988.
Giamatti, A. Bartlett. *The University and the Public Interest.* New York: Atheneum, 1981.
Goodman, Nelson. *Ways of Worldmaking.* Indianapolis: Hackett, 1978.
Gutting, Gary, ed. *The Cambridge Companion to Foucault.* Cambridge, U. K.: Cambridge University Press, 1994.
Gutting, Gary. *Michel Foucault's Archaeology of Scientific Reason.* Cambridge, U. K.: Cambridge University Press, 1989.
Habermas, Jurgen. "Modernity—An Incomplete Project." In *The Anti-Aesthetic: Essays on Postmodern Culture.* Edited by Hal Foster. Port Townsend, Wash.: Bay Press, 1983.
Hall, David L. *Richard Rorty: Prophet and Poet of the New Pragmatism.* Albany: State University of New York Press, 1994.
Harvey, David. *The Condition of Postmodernity.* London: Blackwell, 1989.
Heidegger, Martin. *Basic Writings.* Edited by David Farrell Krell. New York: Harper & Row, 1977.
Hesse, Mary. *Revolutions and Reconstructions in the Philosophy of Science.* Brighton, England: Harvester, 1980.
Holland, John H. *Hidden Order: How Adaptation Builds Complexity.* New York: Addison-Wesley, 1995.
Hutchins, Robert Maynard. *The Conflict in Education in a Democratic Society.* Westport, Conn.: Greenwood Press, 1972. First published 1953.
Hutchins, Robert Maynard. *Education for Freedom.* New York: Grove, 1963. First published 1943.
Hutchins, Robert Maynard. *The Education We Need.* Chicago: Regnery, 1947.
Hutchins, Robert Maynard. *Great Books: the Foundation of a Liberal Education.* New York: Simon and Schuster, 1954.
Hutchins, Robert Maynard. *The Higher Learning in America.* New Haven: Yale University Press, 1936.
Hutchins, Robert Maynard. *The Learning Society.* New York: Praeger, 1968.
Hutchins, Robert Maynard. *The University of Utopia.* Chicago: University of Chicago Press, 1964. First published 1953.
Joyce, Michael. *Of Two Minds: Hypertext Pedagogy and Poetics.* Ann Arbor: University of Michigan Press, 1995.
Kimball, Bruce A. *Orators and Philosophers: A History of the Idea of Liberal Education.* New York: Teachers College Press, 1986.
Klein, Julie Thompson. *Interdisciplinarity: History, Theory, and Practice.* Detroit: Wayne State University Press, 1990.
Kockelmans, Joseph J., ed. *Interdisciplinarity and Higher Education.* University Park, Pa.: Pennsylvania State University Press, 1979.
Kolenda, Konstantin. *Rorty's Humanistic Pragmatism: Philosophy Democratized.* Tampa: University of South Florida Press, 1990.
Kuhn, Thomas S. *The Structure of Scientific Revolutions.* 2d ed., enl. Chicago: University of Chicago Press, 1970. First published 1962.
Kusch, Martin. *Foucault's Strata and Fields: An Investigation into Archaeological and*

Genealogical Science Studies. Dordrecht: Kluwer Academic, 1991.
Lakatos, Imre. "Falsification and the Methodology of Research Programmes." In *Criticism and the Growth of Knowledge.* Edited by Imre Lakatos and Alan Musgrave. Cambridge, U. K.: Cambridge University Press, 1970.
Landow, George P. *Hypertext: the Convergence of Contemporary Critical Theory and Technology.* Baltimore: Johns Hopkins University Press, 1992.
Lawson, Hilary. *Reflexivity: The Post-modern Predicament.* London: Hutchinson, 1985.
Lyotard, Jean-Francois. *The Inhuman: Reflections on Time.* Translated by Geoffrey Bennington and Rachel Bowlby. Cambridge, U. K.: Polity Press, 1991.
Lyotard, Jean-Francois. *The Lyotard Reader.* Edited by Andrew Benjamin. Oxford: Basil Blackwell, 1989.
Lyotard, Jean-Francois. *Political Writings.* Translated by Bill Readings and Kevin Paul Geiman. Minneapolis: University of Minnesota Press, 1993.
Lyotard, Jean-Francois. *The Postmodern Condition: A Report on Knowledge.* Translated by Geoffrey Bennington and Brian Massumi. Minneapolis: University of Minnesota Press, 1984.
Lyotard, Jean-Francois. *The Postmodern Explained: Correspondence 1982–1985.* Edited by Julian Pefanis and Morgan Thomas. Minneapolis: University of Minnesota Press, 1993.
Lyotard, Jean-Francois, and Jean-Loup Thebaud. *Just Gaming.* Translated by Wlad Godzich. Minneapolis: University of Minnesota Press, 1985.
Malachowski, Alan R., ed. *Reading Rorty: Critical Responses* to Philosophy and the Mirror of Nature (and Beyond). Oxford: Basil Blackwell, 1990.
May, Todd. *Between Genealogy and Epistemology: Psychology, Politics, and Knowledge in the Thought of Michel Foucault.* University Park, Pa.: Pennsylvania State University Press, 1993.
McKeachie, Wilbert, Paul Pintrich, Yi-Guang Lin, and David A. F. Smith. *Teaching and Learning in the College Classroom: A Review of Research Literature.* Ann Arbor: National Center for Research to Improve Postsecondary Teaching and Learning, 1986.
Meiland, Jack W. "Concepts of Relative Truth." *Monist* 60, no. 4 (1977): 568–582.
Meiland, Jack W. "On the Paradox of Cognitive Relativism." *Metaphilosophy* 11, no. 2 (April 1980): 115–126.
Meiland, Jack W., and Michael Krausz, eds. *Relativism, Cognitive and Moral.* Notre Dame: University of Notre Dame Press, 1982.
Morris, M., and P. Patton, eds. *Michel Foucault: Power, Truth, Strategy.* Sydney: Feral, 1979.
Mourad, Roger P., Jr. "The Case for Interdisciplinary Knowledge and Practice: A Review of *Interdisciplinarity* and *Rethinking the Curriculum.*" *The Review of Higher Education* 16, no. 2 (Winter 1993): 127–140.
Mulkay, Michael. *Science and the Sociology of Knowledge.* London: George Allen and Unwin, 1979.
Mulkay, Michael. *Sociology of Science: A Sociological Pilgrimage.* Bloomington: Indiana University Press, 1991.
Newman, John Henry. *The Idea of a University Defined and Illustrated*: I. In Nine Discourses Delivered to the Catholics of Dublin [1852]; II. In Occasional Lectures and Essays Addressed to the Members of the Catholic University [1858]. Edited with introduction and notes by I. T. Ker. Oxford: Clarendon, 1976.

Norris, Christopher. *Derrida*. Cambridge, Mass.: Harvard University Press, 1987.
Park, David. *The How and the Why: An Essay on the Origins and Development of Physical Theory*. Princeton: Princeton University Press, 1988.
Passmore, John. *Recent Philosophers*. La Salle, Ill.: Open Court, 1990.
Pelikan, Jaroslav. *The Idea of the University: A Reexamination*. New Haven: Yale University Press, 1992.
Popper, Karl. *The Logic of Scientific Discovery*. London: Hutchinson, 1959.
Putnam, Hilary. *Realism with a Human Face*. Cambridge, Mass.: Harvard University Press, 1990.
Putnam, Hilary. *Renewing Philosophy*. Cambridge, Mass.: Harvard University Press, 1992.
Quine, W. V. O. *From a Logical Point of View*. Cambridge, Mass.: Harvard University Press, 1953.
Rabinow, Paul, ed. *The Foucault Reader*. New York: Pantheon, 1984.
Rand, Richard, ed. *Logomachia: The Conflict of the Faculties*. Lincoln: University of Nebraska Press, 1992.
Rorty, Richard. *Consequences of Pragmatism (Essays: 1972–1980)*. Minneapolis: University of Minnesota Press, 1982.
Rorty, Richard. *Contingency, Irony, and Solidarity*. New York: Cambridge University Press, 1989.
Rorty, Richard. "Education, Socialization, and Individuation." *Liberal Education* 75, no. 4 (September/October 1989): 2–9.
Rorty, Richard. *Essays on Heidegger and Others: Philosophical Papers, Volume 2*. New York: Cambridge University Press, 1991.
Rorty, Richard. "Habermas and Lyotard on Postmodernity." In *Habermas and Modernity*. Edited by Richard Bernstein. Cambridge, Mass.: MIT Press, 1985, pp. 161–175.
Rorty, Richard. *Objectivity, Relativism, and Truth: Philosophical Papers, Volume 1*. New York: Cambridge University Press, 1991.
Rorty, Richard. *Philosophy and the Mirror of Nature*. Princeton: Princeton University Press, 1979.
Rorty, Richard. "Postmodernist Bourgeois Liberalism." In *Hermeneutics and Praxis*. Edited by Robert Hollinger. Notre Dame: University of Notre Dame Press, 1985.
Sallis, John, ed. *Deconstruction and Philosophy: The Texts of Jacques Derrida*. Chicago: University of Chicago Press, 1987.
Schrag, Calvin O. *Communicative Praxis and the Space of Subjectivity*. Bloomington: Indiana University Press, 1986.
Schrag, Calvin O. "Liberal Learning in the Postmodern World." *The Key Reporter* 54, no. 1 (Autumn 1988): 1–4.
Schrag, Calvin O. *Philosophical Papers: Betwixt and Between*. Albany: State University of New York Press, 1994.
Schrag, Calvin O. *Radical Reflection and the Origin of the Human Sciences*. West Lafayette: Purdue University Press, 1980.
Schrag, Calvin O. "Rationality Between Modernity and Postmodernity." In *Lifeworld and Politics: Between Modernity and Postmodernity*. Edited by Stephen K. White. Notre Dame: University of Notre Dame Press, 1989.
Schrag, Calvin O. *The Resources of Rationality: A Response to the Postmodern Challenge*. Bloomington: University of Indiana Press, 1992.

Searle, John. *Intentionality: An Essay in the Philosophy of Mind.* Cambridge, U. K.: Cambridge University Press, 1983.
Searle, John. "Reiterating the Differences: A Reply to Derrida." *Glyph* 1 (1977): 198–208.
Searle, John. "Reply to Louis H. Mackay." *New York Review of Books* 31, no. 1 (1984): 48.
Searle, John. "The World Turned Upside Down." *New York Review of Books* 30, no. 16 (1983): 74–79.
Svinicki, Marilla D. "Practical Implications of Cognitive Theories." In *College Teaching: From Theory to Practice.* Edited by Robert J. Menges and Marilla D. Svinicki. San Francisco: Jossey-Bass, 1991, pp. 27–37.
Tavor Bannet, Eve. *Structuralism and the Logic of Dissent: Barthes, Derrida, Foucault, Lacan.* Urbana: University of Illinois Press, 1989.
Tice, Terrence N., and Thomas P. Slavens. *Research Guide to Philosophy.* Chicago: American Library Association, 1983.
Waldrop, M. Mitchell. *Complexity: The Emerging Science at the Edge of Order and Chaos.* New York: Simon and Schuster, 1992.
Whitehead, Alfred North. *Adventures of Ideas.* New York: Collier Macmillan, 1967. First published 1933.
Whitehead, Alfred North. *The Aims of Education and Other Essays.* New York: Macmillan, 1967. First published 1929.
Whitehead, Alfred North. *The Function of Reason.* Princeton: Princeton University Press, 1929.
Whitehead, Alfred North. *Modes of Thought.* New York: Macmillan, 1938.
Whitehead, Alfred North. *Process and Reality: An Essay in Cosmology.* New York: Macmillan, 1929.
Whitehead, Alfred North. *Science and the Modern World.* New York: Macmillan, 1926.
Wood, David, and Robert Bernasconi, eds. *Derrida and* Differance. Evanston: Northwestern University Press, 1988.

Index

Abnormal, 39–43, 49, 60–61, 70, 93, 97, 101
Alternative foundation. *See* Alternative idea of inquiry; Compelling ideas
Alternative idea of inquiry, 5–6, 8, 33, 42, 49, 55, 60–61, 70–71, 77, 86–89, 91–108
Applied fields, 7–8, 78–79, 81–82, 91–92, 100, 103–4. *See also* Professional fields
Aristotle, 1, 9 n.5, 12, 38, 82, 98

Barthes, Roland, 77
Bernstein, Richard, 6–7

Cavell, Stanley, 106
Cognitive learning theory, 106
Colleges. *See* Universities
Community, 14, 18–19, 20–21, 43, 46, 48, 61–62, 108; intellectual, 7, 9, 14, 21, 31, 36, 41–42, 45–49, 60, 80, 88, 107–8
Compelling ideas, 8–9, 94–108
Complexity theory, 106–7

Davidson, Donald, 39
Democracy, 11, 17–21, 33, 41, 44, 60
Derrida, Jacques, 1, 5–6, 22, 28, 62–70, 105; deconstruction, 62, 67; differance, 66–69; inscription, 65–66, 68–70, presence, 62–66, 68; signification, 63–70; social good, 69; speech, 62–68; writing, 62–70
Descartes, Rene, 38
Dewey, John, 1, 37–38, 40–41
Disciplinary: abnormal ideas, 42; blurring, 84–85, 101; classical, 82–83; compelling ideas, 99–100; constraint, 4–5, 7, 84–88, 104; disparities, 104; dynamic, 83–84; enduring, 98; foundation, 7, 86; fragmentation, 84–85, 101; matrix, 36, 39, 98–99; medieval, 82–83; networks, 103; new disciplines, 85; overdetermination, 99–100; plane, 86–88, 106; postdisciplinary, interaction with, 102–4; preexistent reality, 7, 80–82, 91, 100, 107; progress, 82–84, 97–98; resituation of, 86–88, 92; subdisciplines, 99
Disciplines. *See* Disciplinary

Enlightenment, 2, 11, 29, 88
Epistemology, 37–38, 42, 45, 63
Experience. *See* Compelling ideas; Intellectual activity; Intellectual experience

Feyerabend, Paul, 106

Foucault, Michel, 1, 5–6, 22, 28, 55–62, 70, 91 n.1, 94, 105; changing reality, 59, 61–62; disciplinary technologies, 56–60; episteme, 58–59, 65, 73 n.37; human body, 57, 59; human sciences, 55–59; human subject, 55–61; intellectuals, 59–61; knowledge/power, 55–62; local sites, 56–57, 61; natural sciences, 59; representation, 58–59; social good, 59–61; system, 57, 60–61

Foundation. *See* Alternative idea of inquiry; Disciplinary; Modern inquiry

Gardner, Howard, 106
Goodman, Nelson, 106
Great Books, 12–13, 40
Gadamer, Hans-Georg, 39–40, 48
Giamatti, A. Bartlett, 5, 17–22, 40, 42

Habermas, Jurgen, 2
Hegel, Georg, 30, 64, 67
Heidegger, Martin, 1 n.1, 47–48, 62, 64
Hermeneutic, 39–40, 45–46, 48
Hesse, Mary, 106
Humanities, 19, 40, 78, 81
Humanity, 2, 11, 18, 20–22, 33, 36, 41, 44, 60
Hume, David, 7
Husserl, Edmund, 64
Hutchins, Robert Maynard, 5, 12–15, 17–18, 20–22, 40, 42
Hypermedia, 106

Inquirer as cause, 103–4; anticipation of, 105–7
Inquiry. *See* Modern, inquiry; Post-disciplinary inquiry
Intellectual activity: inquiry, alternative idea of, 8, 81, 83–88, 91, 93, 96, 98, 100, 102–4, 108; inquiry, modern, 81, 83–88; postmodern critique, 6, 33–34, 37, 43, 48, 62, 71
Intellectual experience: compelling ideas, 92–104, 108; modern inquiry, 8, 11, 14–17, 19–20; postmodern critique, 6, 43–44, 48–49, 64

Intellectually compelling ideas. *See* Compelling ideas
Interdisciplinary, 7–8, 22, 32, 35, 42, 46, 77, 81–82, 86–88, 92, 100, 104; institutes, 84–85; particularity, 87. *See also* Disciplinary; Post-disciplinary inquiry

Kant, Immanuel, 7, 38, 45, 64
Knowledge for its own sake, 5, 9, 11, 17–18, 20–22, 31, 33, 35, 42–43, 79, 82, 98
Knowledge its own end. *See* Knowledge for its own sake
Kuhn, Thomas, 30, 39, 93, 106

Lakatos, Imre, 106
Language games, 28–29, 31, 33–36, 40–42, 47
Levi-Strauss, Claude, 3
Liberal education, 13–14, 19, 89 n.2
Local, 32–33, 36–37, 42–43, 45, 56–57, 61, 100–101, 107
Locke, John, 38
Lyotard, Jean-Francois, 1, 6, 22, 28–37, 42–44, 46–48, 55, 58, 60, 70, 97, 105; language games, 28–29, 31, 33–36; legitimation, 29–33; local determinism, 32–33, 36; logical positivism, 30–31; metanarrative, 29–30, 32–33, 36–37; multiplicity, 30, 32, 35, 47; nascence, 28, 34; performativity, 31–32, 35; postmodern condition, 31; pragmatic, 30, 33–34; science, 23–33, 36; social good, 35–37; system, 30–32, 35–36

Meiland, Jack, 106
Modern: absolute foundation, 3; aims, 2, 4–6, 11–22; constraint, 70; disciplines, 82–84, 97–98; inquiry, 4–7, 11, 14, 19, 22, 27; inquiry, basic condition of, 71, 77–86; inquiry, relation to the past, 71, 77, 85, 91, 97–98; limitations, 7, 27; social critique, 3
Modernity, project of, 2, 106. *See also* Modern; Progress

Mulkay, Michael, 106
Multiplicity, 20, 32, 35–36, 42, 44, 56. *See also* Plurality

Nascence, 28, 34, 36, 86
Newman, John Henry, 20–21

Pelikan, Jaroslav, 5, 20–22, 42
Plato, 29, 38, 64
Plurality, 19, 30, 33–34, 47. *See also* Multiplicity
Popper, Karl, 106
Postdisciplinary inquiry, 8–9, 100–108; disciplinary inquiry, interaction with, 102–4; instruction, 105; relation to the past, 102; research, current, 105–6; research programs, 9, 104–5
Postmodern: distinctions, 3–4; relation to the past, 27, 33, 61–62, 71, 77. *See also* Progress, postmodern critique of
Poststructural, 3
Pragmatic, 1, 30, 33–35, 38, 40–41
Preexistent reality: alternative foundation, 7–8, 94–108; disciplinary, 7–8, 80–82, 87–88, 89, 91–92, 98–100, 102–3; modern inquiry, 7–8, 77–80, 88–89, 91–92, 97; postdisciplinary inquiry, 100–108
Professional fields, 7, 22, 78–79, 81, 91–92. *See also* Applied fields
Progress, 2, 4–6, 11–12, 13–22, 79–86, 97–99, 103, 105, 108; postmodern critique of, 27–28, 32–33, 36, 40–41, 44–45, 55–57, 61–63
Putnam, Hilary, 6, 106

Qualitative research, 107
Quantum physics, 106
Quine, W. V. O., 106

Remaking, 39, 41–43, 46, 96
Representation, 37–38, 41, 58–59, 68, 80, 91, 99, 100–102
Rorty, Richard, 1, 6–7, 22, 28, 37–48, 61, 63, 70, 93, 96–97, 105–6; and John Dewey, 1, 37–38, 40–41; edification, 38–40; epistemology, 37–38; hermeneutic, 39–40; languages as tools, 40–42; normal and abnormal discourse, 39–43; pragmatism, 1, 38, 40–41; remaking, 39, 41–43; representation, 37–38, 41; science, 38–40; social good, 41–43
Rousseau, Jean-Jacques, 64

Schrag, Calvin, 1, 6, 22, 28, 44–49, 62, 70, 105; communicative praxis, 45–48; hermeneutic, radical, 45–46, 48; Other, 45–49; science, 44, 46–47; social good, 43, 47–48; transversal reason, 44–49
Science, 2, 6, 11, 13–18, 20–22, 28–33, 36, 38–40, 44, 46–47, 62, 65, 77, 82, 105–6; human, 55–59; natural, 59, 78, 81; philosophy of, 106; social, 47, 78, 81–82; sociology of, 106
Social good, 5, 11, 28, 35–37, 41, 43, 48, 61, 108
System, 15, 30–32, 35–36, 57, 60–61, 65, 68–69, 107–8

Truth, 4, 6–7, 9, 11–15, 18, 20–21, 28–32, 35, 38–39, 41–42, 44, 55–56, 60–64, 66, 69–70, 75 n.70, 89 n.4

University of Berlin, 30
Universities, 2–3, 5, 7–8, 12–14, 17–18, 20–22, 31–33, 36, 47–48, 60–61, 75 n.47, 77–83, 89 n.2, 101, 108

Whitehead, Alfred North, 5, 14–17, 20–22, 40, 42
Williams, Bernard, 6
Wittgenstein, Ludwig, 28, 38

About the Author

ROGER P. MOURAD, JR. is Adjunct Instructor at the University of Michigan.

www.ingramcontent.com/pod-product-compliance
Lightning Source LLC
Chambersburg PA
CBHW070335230426
43663CB00011B/2323